DAVID LITTLEJOHN, the editor of this selection of Samuel Johnson's letters, is a native of San Francisco and a fourth-generation Californian. He did his undergraduate work at the University of California (Berkeley) and then went east for further study at Harvard. After receiving his Ph.D. from Harvard he returned to Berkeley, where he is now Assistant Professor in the Department of English.

MR. LITTLEJOHN's varied interests have led him to write on a broad range of topics: Shakespeare and the Anti-Realist novel, Henry Miller and Edmund Wilson, "On the Banning of Books," Jean Genet, Robinson Jeffers, and F. Scott Fitzgerald. This volume, his first full-length book, will be followed by a study of *Samuel Johnson and the Moral Imagination*, a volume dealing with André Gide, and a book on American Negro writers, *The Literature of the Race War*.

Dr.
JOHNSON

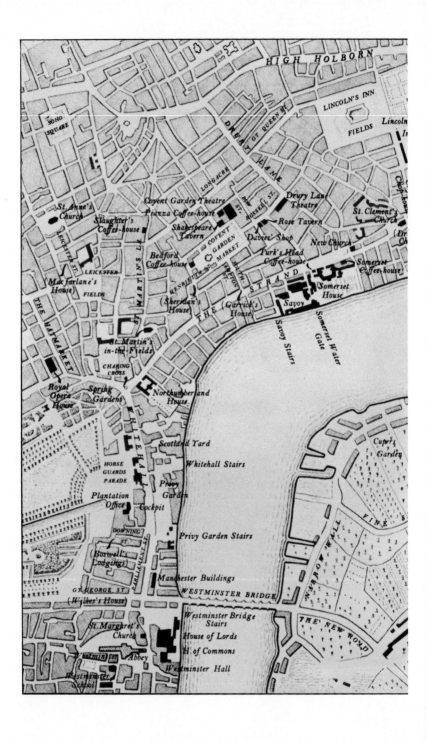

HIGH HOLBORN

SOHO
SQUARE

LINCOLN'S INN

FIELDS   Lincoln
                        I

GT. QUEEN ST.

DRURY LANE

LONGACRE

RUSSELL ST.

Covent Garden Theatre

Piazza Coffee-house

Drury Lane
Theatre

St. Clement's
Church

St. Anne's
Church

Slaughter's
Coffee-house

Shakespeare
Tavern

Rose Tavern

(Dr
Ch

LEICESTER ST.

COVENT
GARDEN
MARKET

Davies' Shop

New Church

Bedford
Coffee-house

Turk's Head
Coffee-house

Somerset
Coffee-house

LEICESTER

(Macfarlane's
House)

FIELDS

HENRIETTA ST.

SOUTH HAMPTON ST.

(Sheridan's
House)

THE

STRAND

Somerset
House

ST. MARTIN'S LANE

(Garrick's
House)

Savoy

Savoy Stairs

Somerset Water Gate

THE HAYMARKET

St. Martin's-
in-the-Fields

CHARING
CROSS

Royal
Opera
House

Spring
Gardens

Northumberland
House.

Cuper's
Garden

Scotland Yard

WHITEHALL

Whitehall Stairs

HORSE
GUARDS
PARADE

Privy
Garden

Plantation
Office

Cockpit

Privy Garden Stairs

DOWNING ST.

FINE

NARROW WALL

(Boswell's
Lodgings)

KING ST.

Manchester Buildings

GT. GEORGE ST.

WESTMINSTER BRIDGE

(Wilkes's House)

Westminster Bridge
Stairs

St. Margret's
Church

House of Lords

H. of Commons

THE NEW ROAD

Westminster Abbey

Westminster Hall

Westminster
School

Dr. JOHNSON

HIS LIFE IN LETTERS

•

SELECTED *and* EDITED *by*

DAVID LITTLEJOHN

Prentice-Hall, Inc. Englewood Cliffs, New Jersey

33,718

CONTENTS

Dr.
JOHNSON

"We talked of Letter-writing. JOHNSON. 'It is now become so much the fashion to publish letters, that in order to avoid it, I put as little into mine as I can.' BOSWELL. 'Do what you will, Sir, you cannot avoid it. Should you even write as ill as you can, your letters would be published as curiosities.'"

INTRODUCTION

by David Littlejohn

There are a number of possible justifications for our prying habit of publishing and reading the private letters of eminent men. In many cases, the letters were not meant to be private; the author had honestly hoped that someone would publish them. The device of a private letter, like the device of a diary, has often served simply as a comfortable way of writing to the world while pretending not to. Letters, secondly, often contain valuable comments on valuable works, on historic events; an author can confess his misgivings, reveal the stages in his progress, judge his own works all in the quiet comfort of a letter. And thinkers, thirdly, have often thought as well and as usefully in the privacy of correspondence as in the publicity of print.

We can appeal to each of these justifications in the case of Samuel Johnson. The celebrated insults to Chesterfield and Macpherson (Letters 19 and 120) were obviously half intended for larger audiences; the letter to "Urban" (7) Johnson published himself. As for "valuable comments," it is surely no mere eavesdropping curiosity to trace, through the letters, the origins of the Dictionary and of *Rasselas*, to follow the *Lives of the Poets* from inception through publication, to read Johnson's own judgments of his *Shakespeare* or his *Journey to the Western Islands*.

And thirdly, Johnsonian wisdom fills these letters, wisdom of both the spontaneous and the more carefully brewed varieties, as beneficial to the last reader as to the first. There are here hundreds of opinions from a man whose every opinion warrants attention. There are letters—not necessarily the most readable—that are little *Ramblers* in themselves, little Essays on Serious Subjects. There are others, like the letters to Baretti, as keen and as palatable as the best of Johnson's public prose. There are judgments on books, poems, plays, and authors, on government policy and the state of the nation. Such texts as Johnson's Scottish letters to Mrs. Thrale (the rough draft of his *Journey to the Western Islands,* 100-108) or his on-the-spot accounts of the Gordon Riots (180-183) ought obviously to be in the public domain. And one can even find a few of the pungent conversational *mots* to be expected of Boswell's hero: "I dined yesterday at Sir Joshua's with Mrs Cholmondeley, and she told me, I was the best critick in the world, and I told her, that nobody in the world could judge like her the merit of a Critick." "You are always complaining of melancholy," he writes to Boswell, "and I conclude from those complaints that you are fond of it. No man talks of that which he is desirous to conceal, and every man desires to conceal that of which he is ashamed."

It is on ground more fundamental, however, and more peculiarly Johnsonian that I would establish my case for this particular invasion of privacy. The case goes back to an interpretation of Johnson, and of Johnson's importance.

Johnson's position in the world of English letters—a position, traditionally, in the very front rank—may appear on consideration to be unearned and indefensible. There are no works, no solid substantial books to back it up. It cannot be alone for any thing he wrote, or even for all the things he wrote, or even for all the things he said added to all the things he wrote that Johnson merits his stance as a sort of neo-classical Colossus straddling English letters. His one "novel," for all its sad truth, hardly merits the name; his great poem falls short of first rank. His political thinking was archaic even in the eighteenth century; his religious thinking is unexceptional. And the moral essay is not a genre from which literary heroes are made. Wise as he was, he was no philosopher, no epoch-turning thinker, no Hume or Voltaire or Rousseau. Even his literary criticism, the most durable and most highly regarded portion of his work, may often seem only an impressive historical curiosity, more a document in the history of thought than a guide of any critical use today.

And yet there he stands. Without a "major work" to his name he has earned his place in the Pantheon. We quote his opinions on every conceivable subject, as if he were some sacred oracle, some early

Church Father; he is a man with whom, according to T. S. Eliot, it is dangerous to disagree. People who have not read one word of his writing know who he is. Generations have read his biography.

It is not so much what he wrote that matters, or even what he said; but rather what he was, what he so solidly and irreducibly was. Johnson is important, first, not as a writer or thinker, but as a fact, as a human phenomenon, as a full and charged instance of life. He is the one example in English history or English literature of a man who has earned his pre-eminent place by simply and supremely being what he was—and then letting someone else take copious note of that extraordinary fact. Of no other man of letters can it so positively be said that his greatest work is his Life.

This is not to say that his thoughts, of themselves, may not be independently prized. Certain of his perceptions of moral psychology, his insights into the human heart, have been unequalled by any other thinker's; scores of his literary verdicts are unlikely ever to be displaced; his conversational wisdom has endowed us with hundreds of quotations. But it is next to impossible to regard them independently: all of Johnson seems to be present in his every remark. We feel his presence, hear his voice as we never do, say, Aristotle's or Emerson's or Coleridge's. Which only proves (and how well Boswell understood it) how totally and exactly the writings, the sayings are a function of the larger and livelier thing that is Johnson himself. It is to this, to all of it, that we must direct our attention.

The sum of human fact called Samuel Johnson can be better experienced than described. What it is *not* is any one of the several Johnsons commonly extracted for analysis—the brilliantly pushy arguer of Boswell's portrait, the sufferer of the *Prayers and Meditations*, the convincing critical empiricist, the dark moral sage. All of these must be somehow fused, resynthesized into a single experience. And the way to do it is to immerse oneself willfully and wholeheartedly in the literary remains.

To the fact that is Johnson every scrap contributes; by it, conversely, is every scrap justified. And this includes the letters. We begin with Boswell's account; we fill in, we shape the contours with the records of other contemporaries, Mrs. Thrale, Fanny Burney,

Sir John Hawkins. This gives us the vividly detailed external image, the walking and talking Johnson, together with a clear outline of the life. We turn then to Johnson's own public writings—*The Vanity of Human Wishes, Rasselas,* the essays, the *Lives of the Poets,* all the little prefaces and poems and dedications; and the experience, our experience of this human event, begins to take on a depth and objective extension. Finally, impelled by all these, we look to the private writings—the diaries and annals, the prayers and meditations, the letters—hoping to find the spark that will set it all in motion.

If you have followed such a progress, you will need no encouragement to read the letters. You know already how and why Johnson is important; you will have already been magnetized, polarized, half repelled and half attracted by this odd specimen of larger-than-life-sized humanity. You will read the letters, dull, pompous, trivial, whatever they may be, because you know the man and want to know him better. You are, in a word, becoming a Johnsonian.

But if, on the other hand, you are neither so well equipped nor so kindly disposed, if you have come to the letters early and unpossessed of the full image of their author, they can help you to attain it. These letters are not just the bits and scraps that a great man leaves in his wake; they are a part, an essential part, of that storehouse of documentation that creates, for us, the experience of his greatness.

For his is not an historical greatness, or even (as we have seen) a literary one. It is a human greatness, a *grandeur de l'homme;* and it depends on these documented evidences of his humanness. He is what the French, having so many, call an "Exemplary Man"; a man whose whole life, whose moral presence, whose quality and bearing and depth as a man are his claim to greatness. Such a man's deeds and writings will count, of course, as aspects of that life; but he is no mere actor or "artist." The French, as I say, have had many such men: André Gide is the perfect type; or Pascal, Rousseau, Victor Hugo, Camus. Since Johnson may well be the *only* real *homme exemplaire* of the English-speaking world, he is all the more tenaciously to be prized.

This does not mean that Johnson should be thought of as any-

thing so petty as a moral "example"; he could never be scaled down
to fit the part. He is wise, benevolent, penetrating, long-suffering,
yes—all hugely, gigantically. But he is also mean, idiosyncratic,
prejudiced, cruel—and all these gigantically too. He is one of the
largest and most complete human beings that ever lived; the world's
content of life was measurably increased by his being in it. Consider
only his titanic struggles against disease, against madness, against
death-wishing lethargy, against death itself.

The "storehouse of documentation" is no accident. Men came
to see him like a Pyramid, to hear him like an oracle. They recog-
nized in Johnson a singular phenomenon, and felt compelled to
record it. For us, discovering him through these records, his own
writings as well as others' about him, he is more of an experience
than an example: a continuing, inexhaustible experience of so vast
and so energetic and so various a human phenomenon that we are
certain, however much and however strongly we may resist and
disagree, to be charged ourselves, to be energized and expanded by
the encounter.

These letters fall somewhere between the journals and the essays,
between the writings wholly private and those wholly public, being
neither quite so intimate as the one nor so studied as the other.
They are broadcast across the full range between impersonal objec-
tivity and open self-revelation. Let me briefly survey the letters,
grouping them somewhat arbitrarily into categories across this wide
range, to see what they can contribute toward an understanding
of Johnson; and to estimate, at the same time, what additional and
purely "literary" benefits they may afford.

At one extreme are the moral essays, the sententiously impersonal
lay sermons; I have included few examples of these. They are more
strained, for some reason, than the periodical essays they resemble.
(See Letter 57, the first to Boswell.) Better—in fact, occasionally
sublime—are the letters of comfort and condolence, a sub-genre at
which Johnson may well be the master in our language. See the
deathbed series to Hill Boothby (22-26) and to his mother (36-41);
the letters to Elphinston (9, 163); to Mrs. Thrale (138 and 196); the
single perfect line to Garrick's widow (167). Equally fine are John-

son's formal letters of purpose, those letters of petition and thanksgiving for which the rhythms and tone of the high Johnsonian style are so perfectly suited.

Next come Johnson's "journalistic" reports, distinctly unlike those of his century's most famous correspondent, Horace Walpole. The unpolished straightforwardness of Johnson's epistolary journalism contrasts markedly with Walpole's brilliance and wit. The two often describe the same scenes and events, and it is interesting to compare their responses. Johnson was a somewhat cumbersome traveler; his one good eye could, at times, go dull when observing Society too closely. His accounts of the theatre, of London high life, of country society, we must admit, acquire most of their delight from our knowledge of the narrator. His record of the 1780 riots has more strength than color. His tales of the Highlands and Hebrides are readable only *despite* a certain generalized spareness. Again, it is Johnson's participation (and hence ours) that gives life to the reports. He was not the quick-eyed slippery sort, and his very unfitness for the journalist's task often elicits our sympathy and delight.

Johnson's passing comments on the world of affairs, the Great World beyond his immediate concerns, are quite another matter. It is always instructive to have so central an observation post on history, to have the hero himself describe his setting. He provides us with a roll call of new books and plays, ticking each off as it arrives: *Clarissa, Evelina, She Stoops to Conquer*, Crabbe's *The Village*, Percy's *Reliques*. He recounts the successes of his friends Garrick and Reynolds, of the Club members generally. One may trace through his letters, his high Tory letters, the disastrous turns of political history in eighteenth-century England. He notes the arrival of George III; the Seven Years' War, with England's qualified victory; Burke's entry into politics; the whole calamitous American episode (including his own wars with the Patriots); the fears of a French invasion; the fall of North in 1782, of Rockingham's group soon after; Pitt's scandalous Reform Bill in 1783. He laments throughout, in the manner of Walpole, the decaying state of England—and provides (Letter 189) an interesting instance of one of the causes of decay.

6

All of these letters, beside their special delights, tell us something of Johnson. But more to the point, since "the experience of Johnson" is my basic defense for this series, are those that reveal character directly. Such letters offer pages of living evidence for the quality of his religious orthodoxy, of his political opinions, of his moral beliefs; for his desperate fears of death and aloneness and insanity, for the "vile melancholy" that became his personal plague. We learn of his healths and sicknesses, his joys and despairs, of his secret benevolence; in the strange French letter to Mrs. Thrale (95) we have suggestions of the most radical disorder. In the very tone of his personal letters, the exact and subtle variations between his words to one correspondent and his words to another, we learn worlds about his friendships and personal needs: we can measure precisely the degrees of intimacy and distance.

To his "honoured Mother," for example, he is the distant and dutiful son. To the dying Hill Boothby he is the ardently Christian lover, all his passion sublimed into prayer. With Boswell he can remonstrate in fatherly-friendly fashion, perhaps consciously trying to fill the place of an alienated parent. But though he tells all, or almost all, to his biographer, his heart is never quite open; a slight chill hangs about their correspondence, a chill rarely felt in their conversations. (When age and solitude press too heavily, the old warmth returns: "Come to me, my dear Bozzy, and let us be as happy as we can. We will go again to the Mitre, and talk old times over.")

Mrs. Thrale hears him in every mood, a fruit of their intense and complex relationship. Most often his way with her is that of a gay, good-natured wit and allusiveness that presume a vast fund of common experience cosily shared. "We make a hard shift here to live on without a regatta," he writes to her from Lichfield, as she frolics in town.

One can distinguish easily between his letters to Lucy, his simple spinster stepdaughter, and those to the clergyman-squire Taylor, rich and dull: to both, though, he must write with a kind of primer simplicity, designed to meet their own narrowness and denseness; with both he can forget that he is a celebrity, drop all stylistic pretensions, and compare aches and pains with a common countryman's directness. And to eight-year-old Queeney Thrale he is the perfect little girl's beau. "You said nothing of Lucy, I suppose she is grown a pretty good scholar, and a very good playfellow; after dinner we shall have good sport playing all together, and we will none of us cry."

What this collection is especially designed to reveal, however, is not so much the static portrait-in-depth of a personality, with all its quirks and virtues and obsessions and ideas, as the dynamic, dramatic arc of a career. It is the progress, the slow rise and the agonizing, long, difficult decline I have especially tried to trace, marking by key letters each of the intersections that mattered.

Over 1500 surviving letters have been reduced to 246; and even these were stripped of much superfluous stuff, so as to inscribe on the reader's memory the stark pattern of a life with its lights and deep shadows, its jolting ups and downs. One follows, through the hero's own words, the gradual expansion and contraction of a primarily literary life; the milestones are books, strained out by convulsive efforts year after year. Friends join us on the way, then drop off and die, and he marks in his letters each sad passing, like a bell, tolling the hours. Boswell comes in "with his noisy benevolence," in 1763; the Thrales come and go. From the years of struggle and debt, through the pension and Streatham and years of social comfort, to the drab years of loneliness, we watch Johnson fighting on, as body and brain, both mined with diseases, gradually begin to give way. On go the dull cycles of visits, the empty letters year after year from Lichfield to London, from London to Lichfield: "I was glad to go abroad, and, perhaps, glad to come home; which is, in other words, I was, I am afraid, weary of being at home, and weary of being abroad." And then, the last three years; the blows before the end fall frequently and hard.

April 4, 1781: "Mr. Johnson knows that Sir Joshua Reynolds and the other Gentlemen will excuse his incompliance with the Call, when they are told that Mr. Thrale died this morning."

January 17, 1782: "Our old friend Mr Levett, who was last night eminently cheerful, died this morning."

June 17, 1783: "It hath pleased almighty God this morning to deprive me of the powers of speech."

September 9, 1783: " 'Mrs. Williams, from mere inanition, has at length paid the last debt to Nature, about 3 o'clock this morning.' "

September 24, 1783: "My case, which you guessed at not amiss, is a Sarcocele; a dreadful disorder which however, I hope, God will not suffer to destroy me."

July 2, 1784, to Mrs. Thrale: "If I interpret your letter right, you are ignominiously married. . . ."

Some letters of interest I have had to exclude, but the great bulk of those dropped were duplications or commonplace trifles: social chatterings, accounts of his health, summer notes from the country. The distribution of surviving letters falls heavily on the later years: there are no letters before 1730, only 39 for the next 20 years; there are 460 for the final three years of Johnson's life. One has, reasonably enough, a more active urge to preserve the letters of a celebrity than those of a friend who has not yet arrived. I have tried to even the spread somewhat, but it is difficult, and it would be wrong, to erase entirely the emphasis on the dying Johnson; this, after all, is when he had most time and inclination to write.

Deletions from the letters are not censorings: I have always tried to save the most interesting material. Johnson shared with the rest of us the bad habit of beginning his letters with letter-writer's cant (Thanks for your last letter, Why I haven't written sooner, and so on), which we can dispense with. Where no address is given, it may be presumed to be London, or (on rare occasions) unknown.

The text of the letters is taken from *The Letters of Samuel Johnson*, collected and edited by R. W. Chapman in three volumes, at the Clarendon Press, Oxford, 1952; acknowledgment is here gratefully made to the Delegates of the Clarendon Press for its use. None of the letters unearthed since Dr. Chapman's edition seemed to merit inclusion. Spelling, capitalization, punctuation, and language are all Johnson's, except where slips or uncertainties have made correction or conjecture advisable. Johnson's punctuation (and sometimes spelling) is confessedly bizarre. But the slight extra effort it will take to interpret seems warranted by that extra inch of personality it reveals, that hint it offers of the natural rhythms of his speaking voice.

The linking commentaries between the letters, it is hoped, provide the connective tissue necessary to make of them a continuously readable narrative. Together with the footnotes, they should answer most questions the letters may raise, and create a background of understanding without interrupting or distracting the reader. Only in the section on the Scottish Tour have I indulged in "unnecessary" footnoting, to share something of the fun of a simultaneous reading of Johnson's and Boswell's accounts. Correspondents and other characters are identified in an index at the back. I have made use, among other sources, of Chapman's notes to the *Letters*, the notes to the Hill-Powell Boswell, the Yale edition of Johnson's *Diaries, Prayers, and Annals*, and the biographical works of James L. Clifford and Joseph Wood Krutch for my summaries and notes. For the fine photograph on the cover of Johnson's statue at St. Clement Dane's, London, I am indebted to Mr. Allyn Baum of New York. I should like to thank The McGraw-Hill Book Company of New York for permission to reprint the map of Johnson's London from their edition of Boswell's *London Journal*; and especially, Mr. and Mrs. Donald F. Hyde of North Branch, New Jersey, for their gracious permission to copy two manuscript letters of Johnson's from their collection.

To 1755

Johnson's public career began in *1737*, when he came up to London from the country, sharing a horse with David Garrick, "with two-pence half-penny in my pocket," as he later told the story. He was already twenty-seven; he had made no sure beginning, and had reason to be anxious. He had tried bookselling in his father's shop at Lichfield, writing and translating for the Birmingham press, teaching school (for three prison-like months), and running a school of his own. Each failure was more bleak than the last.

Family circumstances had forced him to leave Oxford in *1729* after just thirteen months, to relinquish his high ambitions for a gentleman's career. He had fallen, after this disappointment, into a desperate melancholy, a near-suicidal despair for almost two years—a *condition he was never quite able to escape. Moving briefly to Birmingham, he applied, constantly and in vain, for new teaching posts, for writing jobs of various kinds.*

In July of 1735 he had married Elizabeth ("Tetty") Porter, the widow of a Birmingham dry goods merchant and mother of three. He was then twenty-five, a diseased but vigorous man; she was forty-six, and aging fast. Friends were surprised, relatives were scandalized; readers and scholars, after two hundred years, are still a bit nonplussed. Johnson's seventeen years with Tetty were, to say the least, edgy; but he insisted it was a "love match," and the one surviving letter gives evidence of both sympathy and alienation.

Once in London, Johnson quickly won the confidence of the archetypical hard-boiled editor, Edward Cave of the Gentleman's Magazine. *Planting Tetty in a succession of houses, he spent the next seven years churning out poems, essays, translations, reviews, biographies, and Parliamentary reports for Cave with the best of the Grub Street hacks, never lifting himself and his wife very far from poverty and obscurity. His poem* London *brought ten pounds, or about ten-pence a line; the famous* Life of Savage *fifteen guineas. "No man but a blockhead ever wrote, except for money."*

In 1746, after nine years in London, Johnson—now thirty-six— was nowhere near fame, and light-years from fortune. His domestic trials increased as Tetty aged and sickened and soured; there is evidence of long separations. The Lichfield mortgage was three years overdue. He took to writing prefaces, dedications, and sermons for friends; he considered the Law; he thought up lists of great literary projects, including an edition of Shakespeare, none of which came to light. There seemed to be no way out.

It was at this barren, near-desperate stage that the greatest of his literary projects—the Dictionary—was first proposed. His reputation, at least among the booksellers, was sufficient for them to recognize in him the only man in England equipped to undertake so historic and formidable a work. They offered him over £1500; he spent it all and more, long before he was done. He estimated it would take three years: it took nine, nine years of mountainous, awesome drudgery, for a man who thought himself "the most indolent man in Britain." But when it was finished his name was made

—The Lexicographer, "Dictionary Johnson"—and his place secure. During the Dictionary Years (1746-55), Johnson wrote also his one great poem, The Vanity of Human Wishes, *and most of the 208* Rambler *essays, both of which sounded his bass chord of misery, of a heavy, deep, world-weary melancholy. Tetty's death on March 18, 1752—a day he was to commemorate in his prayers ever after— helped to fix this tone, and left him in a state of guilt-ridden, moody loneliness he was to spend the rest of his life trying to avoid. Among his other miscellaneous writings were twenty-nine* Adventurers *for Hawkesworth. He met young Bennet Langton, an admirer of his* Ramblers, *the painter Reynolds and the novelist Richardson, and, measurably lower on the social scale but no less important to Johnson, his lifelong housemates Levett and Williams and his Negro servant Frank. His tragedy* Irene, *written in 1738, finally opened at Garrick's Drury Lane Theatre in 1749 (though no great critical or popular success, it did bring Johnson £300) and Johnson bought a new scarlet and gold-lace outfit for the occasion.*

But for the most part the nine years were spent in the garret of the house at 17 Gough Square, off Fleet Street, toiling away at the Dictionary with his assistants. In February of 1755 he could at last write to Thomas Warton, "I now begin to see land"; and, in what Boswell called "the celebrated letter"—perhaps Johnson's most famous—he could proudly reject Lord Chesterfield's belated and stingy support. In April, he held in his hands the two thick, heavy folio volumes labeled "Johnson's Dictionary." The Grub Street days were nearing an end.

1. To Edward Cave

Lichfield, November 25, 1734

Sir

As You appear no less sensible than your Readers of the defects of your Poetical Article, you will not be displeased, if, in order to the improvement of it, I communicate to You the Sentiments of a person,[1] who will undertake on reasonable terms sometimes to fill a column.

His opinion is, that the Publick would not give You a bad reception, if beside the current Wit of the Month, which a critical examination would generally reduce to a narrow Compass, You admitted not only Poems, Inscriptions &c never printed before, which he will sometimes supply You with; but likewise short literary Dissertations in Latin or English, Critical Remarks on Authours Ancient or Modern, forgotten Poems that deserve Revival, or loose pieces, like Floyers, worth preserving. By this Method your Literary Article, for so it might be call'd, will, he thinks, be better recommended to the Publick, than by low Jests, awkward Buffoonery, or the dull Scurrilities of either Party.

If such a Correspondence will be agreeable to You, be pleased to inform me in two posts, what the Conditions are on which You shall expect it. Your late offer[2] gives me no reason to distrust your Generosity. If You engage in any Literary projects beside this Paper, I have other designs to impart if I could be secure from having others reap the advantage of what I should hint.

Your letter, by being directed to S. Smith to be left at the Castle in Birmingham, Warwackshire, will reach

Your humble Servant.

2. *To Richard Congreve, Oxford*

Great Haywood, June 25, 1735

Dear Sir . . .

I am now going to furnish a House in the Country, and keep a private boarding-school for Young Gentlemen whom I shall endeavour to instruct in a method somewhat more rational than those commonly practised which you know there is no great vanity in presuming to attempt. Before I draw up my plan of Education, I shall attempt to procure an account of the different ways of teach-

[1] The "person" is Johnson himself. "S. Smith," to whom Cave was to reply, is fictitious.
[2] Cave had recently offered a £50 prize for the best poem submitted on "Life, Death, Judgement, Heaven, and Hell."

ing in use at the most celebrated Schools, and shall therefore hope You will favour me with the method of the Charterhouse, and procure me that of Westminster.

It may be written in a few lines by only mentioning under each class their Exercise and Authours. . . .

3. *To Edward Cave*

(*1738*)

Sir

When I took the liberty of writing to you a few days ago, I did not expect a repetition of the same pleasure so soon; for a pleasure I shall always think it to converse in any manner with an ingenious and candid man; but having the inclosed poem[3] in my hands to dispose of for the benefit of the author (of whose abilities I shall say nothing, since I send you his performance), I believed I could not procure more advantageous terms from any person than from you, who have so much distinguished yourself by your generous encouragement of poetry; and whose judgement of that art nothing but your commendation of my trifle can give me any occasion to call in question. I do not doubt but you will look over this poem with another eye, and reward it in a different manner, from a mercenary bookseller, who counts the lines he is to purchase, and considers nothing but the bulk. I cannot help taking notice, that, besides what the author may hope for on account of his abilities, he has likewise another claim to your regard, as he lies at present under very disadvantageous circumstances of fortune. I beg therefore that you will favour me with a letter to-morrow, that I may know what you can afford to allow him, that he may either part with it to you, or find out (which I do not expect) some other way more to his satisfaction.

I have only to add, that as I am sensible I have transcribed it very coarsely, which, after having altered it, I was obliged to do, I will, if you please to transmit the sheets from the press, correct it for you; and will take the trouble of altering any stroke of satire which you may dislike.

[3] *London*. The anonymous "author" is again Johnson.

By exerting on this occasion your usual generosity, you will not only encourage learning, and relieve distress, but (though it be in comparison of the other motives of very small account) oblige in a very sensible manner,

Sir,

Your very humble servant,

Sam. Johnson.

4. *To Edward Cave*

(*1738*)

Sir

I am extremely obliged by your kind letter, and will not fail to attend you to-morrow with Irene,[4] who looks upon you as one of her best friends.

I was to day with Mr Dodsley, who declares very warmly in favour of the paper you sent him, which he desires to have a share in, it being, as he says, *a creditable thing to be concerned in.*[5] I knew not what answer to make till I had consulted you, nor what to demand on the Author's part, but am very willing that, if you please, he should have a part in it, as he will undoubtedly be more diligent to disperse and promote it. If you can send me word to-morrow what I shall say to him, I will settle matters, and bring the Poem with me for the press, which, as the town empties, we cannot be too quick with.

I am,

Sir, yours, &c.

Sam. Johnson.

---

[4] Johnson's tragedy *Irene* was not produced until 1749.
[5] Dodsley eventually bought the full rights to Johnson's poem for ten pounds.

16

5. To Mrs. Elizabeth Johnson

Lichfield, January 31, 1740[6]

Dearest Tetty

After hearing that You are in so much danger, as I apprehend from a hurt on a tendon, I shall be very uneasy till I know that You are recovered, and beg that You will omit nothing that can contribute to it, nor deny Yourself any thing that may make confinement less melancholy. You have already suffered more than I can bear to reflect upon, and I hope more than either of us shall suffer again. One part at least I have often flatterd myself we shall avoid for the future, our troubles will surely never separate us more. If M does not easily succeed in his endeavours, let him not scruple to call in another Surgeon to consult with him, You may have two or three visits from Ranby or Shipton, who is said to be the best, for a Guinea, which You need not fear to part with on so pressing an occasion, for I can send you twenty pouns more on Monday, which I have received this night; I beg therefore that You will more regard my happiness, than to expose Yourself to any hazards. I still promise myself many happy years from your tenderness and affection, which I sometimes hope our misfortunes have not yet deprived me of. David [7] wrote to me this day on the affair of Irene, who is at last become a kind of Favourite among the Players, Mr Fletewood promises to give a promise in writing that it shall be the first next season, if it cannot be introduced now, and Chetwood the Prompter is desirous of bargaining for the copy, and offers fifty Guineas for the right of printing after it shall be played. I hope it will at length reward me for my perplexities.

Of the time which I have spent from thee, and of my dear Lucy[8] and other affairs, my heart will be at ease on Monday to give Thee a particular account, especially if a Letter should inform me that thy Leg is better, for I hope You do not think so unkindly of me as to imagine that I can be at rest while I believe my dear Tetty in pain.

[6] Johnson spent six months this winter—one of the coldest in England's history—visiting about the country on his own, while Tetty stayed at London. He was not to return to her till March or April.
[7] Garrick.
[8] Lucy Porter.

Be assured, my dear Girl, that I have seen nobody in these rambles upon which I have been forced, that has not contribute to confirm my esteem and affection for thee, though that esteem and affection only contributed to increase my unhappiness when I reflected that the most amiable woman in the world was exposed by my means to miseries which I could not relieve.

I am

My charming Love Yours

Sam: Johnson

Lucy always sends her Duty and my Mother her service.

6. *To Edward Cave*

(*Autumn, 1743*)

Sir

I believe I am going to write a long Letter, and have therefore taken a whole Sheet of Paper. . . .

I am of your opinion with regard to placing most of the resolutions &c in the Margin, and think we shall give the most complete account of Parliamentary proceedings that can be contrived. The Naked Papers without an Historical treatise interwoven, require some other Book to make them understood. I will date the succeeding parts with some exactness but, I think in the margin. You told me on Saturday that I had received money on this work and I find set down 13L 2-6. reckoning the half Guinea, of last Saturday, as you hinted to me that you had many calls for Money. I would not press you too hard, and therefore shall desire only as I send it in two Guineas for a sheet of Copy the rest you may pay me when it shall be more convenient, and even by this sheet payment I shall for some time be very expensive.

The Life of Savage I am ready to go upon and in great Primer and Pica Notes reckon on sending in half a sheet a day, but the money for that shall likewise lye by in your hands till it is done.

With the debates shall I not have business enough? If I had but good Pens.—Towards Mr Savage's Life what more have you got? I would willingly have his tryal &c and know whether his Defence be at Bristol, and would have his Collection of Poems on account of

the Preface—The Plain Dealer—All the Magazins that have anything of his or relating to him. I thought my Letter would be long
but it is now, ended and

I am, Sir

Your &c.

Sam: Johnson

The Boy found me writing this almost in the dark, when I could
not quite easily read yours, I have read the Latin—nothing in it is
well.

I had no notion of having anything for the Inscription, I hope you
don't think I kept it to extort a price. I could think on nothing till
today. If you could spare me another Guinea for the Hist I should
take it very kindly tonight, but if you do not shall not think it an
injury.—I am almost well again—

7. *To Mr. Urban*[9]

(*August 1743*)

Mr Urban

As your Collections show how often you have owed the Orna-
ments of your poetical Pages, to the Correspondence of the unfortunate and ingenious Mr *Savage,* I doubt not but you have so much
regard to his Memory as to encourage any design that may have a
tendency to the Preservation of it from Insults or Calumnies, and
therefore with some Degree of Assurance intreat you to inform the
Publick, that his Life will speedily be published by a Person who was
favoured with his Confidence, and received from himself an Account
of most of the Transactions which he proposes to mention to the
Time of his Retirement to *Swansey* in *Wales.*

From that Period to his Death in the prison of *Bristol,* the Account will be continued from materials still less liable to Objection,
his own Letters and those of his Friends; some of which will be inserted in the Work, and Abstracts of others subjoined in the Margin.

It may be reasonably imagined that others may have the same Design, but as it is not credible that they can obtain the same Materials,

[9] "Sylvanus Urban" was Cave's *nom de plume* as editor; this letter
is a formal advertisement inserted in the *Gentleman's Magazine.*

it must be expected they will supply from Invention the want of Intelligence, and that under the Title of the Life of *Savage* they will publish only a Novel filled with romantick Adventures, and imaginary Amours. You may therefore perhaps gratify the Lovers of Truth and Wit by giving me leave to inform them in your Magazine, that my Account will be published in 8vo by Mr *Roberts* in *Warwick-lane.*

8. *To Thomas Longman*

June 1746

Sir

The Contract fairly engrossed was sent to me yesterday, I suppose by Mr Knaptons direction who is out of town.[10] I should think it a favour if You and the rest of the Gentlemen would breakfast with me that we may sign. If You will appoint a day and write a note to the rest, the Bearer will take it to each of them, or if any other place be more convenient, the writings shall be brought wherever You shall desire by,

Sir,
Your humble Servant
Sam: Johnson

At the golden Anchor near Holbourn Bars

9. *To James Elphinston, Edinburgh*

September 25, 1750

Dear Sir

You have, as I find by every kind of evidence, lost an excellent mother; and I hope you will not think me incapable of partaking of your grief. I have a mother now eighty-two years of age, whom therefore I must soon lose, unless it please God that she rather should mourn for me. I read the letters in which you relate your mother's death to Mrs. Strahan; and think I do myself honour when I tell you that I read them with tears; but tears are neither to me nor to you

[10] The original contract for his *Dictionary of the English Language* was dated June 18, 1746.

of any farther use, when once the tribute of nature has been paid. The business of life summons us away from useless grief, and calls us to the exercise of those virtues of which we are lamenting our deprivation. The greatest benefit which one friend can confer upon another, is to guard, and incite, and elevate his virtues. This your mother will still perform, if you diligently preserve the memory of her life, and of her death: a life, so far as I can learn, useful, wise,[11] and innocent; and a death resigned, peaceful, and holy. I cannot forbear to mention, that neither reason nor revelation denies you to hope, that you may encrease her happiness by obeying her precepts; and that she may, in her present state, look with pleasure, upon every act of virtue to which her instructions or example have contributed. Whether this be more than a pleasing dream, or a just opinion of separate spirits, is indeed of no great importance to us, when we consider ourselves as acting under the eye of God: yet surely there is something pleasing in the belief, that our separation from those whom we love is merely corporeal; and it may be a great incitement to virtuous friendship, if it can be made probable, that that union which has received the divine approbation, shall continue to eternity.

There is one expedient, by which you may, in some degree, continue her presence. If you write down minutely what you remember of her from your earliest years, you will read it with great pleasure, and receive from it many hints of soothing recollection, when time shall remove her yet farther from you, and your grief shall be matured to veneration. To this, however painful for the present, I cannot but advise you, as to a source of comfort and satisfaction in the time to come; for all comfort and all satisfaction, is sincerely wished you by,

Dear Sir,

Your most obliged, most obedient, and most humble servant,

Sam. Johnson.

---

[11] The word may have been "pious." (Chapman.)

10. To Samuel Richardson

March 9, 1751

Dear Sir

   Though Clarissa wants no help from external Splendour I was glad to see her improved in her appearance but more glad to find that she was now got above all fears of prolixity, and confident enough of success, to supply whatever had been hitherto suppressed.[12] I never indeed found a hint of any such defalcation, but I fretted: for though the Story is long, every letter is short.

   I wish you would add an *Index Rerum*, that when the reader recollects any incident he may easily find it, which at present he cannot do, unless he knows in which volume it is told; For Clarissa is not a performance to be read with eagerness and laid aside for ever, but will be occasionally consulted by the busy, the aged, and the studious, and therefore I beg that this Edition by which I suppose Posterity is to abide, may want nothing that can facilitate its use.

I am Sir
Your obliged humble Servant
Sam: Johnson

11. To John Newbery

April 18, 1751

Dear Sir

   I have just now a demand upon me for more money than I have by me: if you could conveniently help me with two pounds, it will be a favour, to

Sir,
Your most humble servant,
Sam: Johnson

---

[12] The so-called fourth edition of Richardson's *Clarissa*, in the "improved" octavo size, was published at this time. Some earlier suppressions were restored.

12. To John Newbery

July 29, 1751

Sir

I beg the favour of you to send me by the bearer, a guinea, for which I will account to you on some future production.

I am, Sir,
Your humble servant,
Sam: Johnson

13. To John Newbery

August 24, 1751

Dear Sir,

I beg the favour of you to lend me another guinea, for which I shall be glad of any opportunity to account with you, as soon as any proper thing can be thought on, or which I will repay you in a few weeks.

I am, Sir,
Your most humble servant
Sam: Johnson.

14. To William Strahan

Dear Sir

I must desire you to add to your other civilities this one, to go to Mr Millar and represent to him our manner of going on, and inform him that I know not how to manage, I pay three and twenty shillings a week to my assistants, in truth without having much assistance from them, but they tell me they shall be able to fall better in method, as indeed I intend they shall. The point is to get two Guineas for

Your humble Servant
Sam: Johnson

15. To John Taylor, Westminster

March 18, 1752

Dear Sir

Let me have your Company and your Instruction. Do not live away from me. My Distress is great.

Pray desire Mrs. Taylor to inform me what mourning I should buy for my Mother and Miss Porter, and bring a note in writing with you.

Remember me in your Prayers—for vain is the help of man.[13]

I am Dear Sir &c.

Sam: Johnson

16. To Joseph Warton

March 8, 1753

Dear Sir

I ought to have written to you before now, but I ought to do many things which I do not, nor can I indeed claim any merit from this Letter, for being desired by the Authours and Proprietor of the Adventurer to look out for another hand, my thoughts necessarily fixed upon you, whose fund of Literature will enable You to assist them with very little interruption of your Studies.

They desire you to engage to furnish one paper a month, at two guineas a paper, which you may very easily perform. We have considered that a Paper should consist of Pieces of Imagination, pictures of Life, and Disquisitions of Literature. The part which depends on the Imagination is very well supplied as you will find when you read the papers; for Descriptions of Life there is now a treaty almost made with an Authour and an Authoress, and the Province of Criticism and Literature they are very desirous to assign to the Commentator on Virgil.

I hope this proposal will not be rejected, and that the next post will bring us your Compliance. I speak as one of the fraternity

---

[13] Tetty died on March 17. Johnson's epitaph for her, written only two weeks before his own death, is given in Letter 244.

though I have no part in the paper beyond now and then a Motto,[14] but two of the Writers are my particular Friends, and I hope the pleasure of seeing a third united to them, will not be denied to dear Sir

Your most obedient and most humble Servant

Sam: Johnson

17. *To Thomas Warton, Oxford*

December 21, 1754

Dear Sir

I am extremely sensible of the favour done me both by Mr. Wise and yourself.[15] The Book cannot, I think, be printed in less than six weeks, nor probably so soon, and I will keep back the titlepage for such an insertion as you seem to promise me. Be pleased to let me know, what money I should send you for bearing the expence of the affair and I will take care that you may have it ready in your hand.

I had lately the favour of a Letter from your Brother with some account of poor Collins for whom I am much concerned: I have a notion that by very great temperance or more properly abstinence he might yet recover.[16]

There is an Old English and Latin book of poems by Barclay called the *Ship* of *Fools*, at the end of which are a number of *Eglogues* (so he writes it from Ægloga) which are probably the first in our Language. If you cannot find the book I will get Mr Dodsly to send it you.

I shall be extremely glad to hear from you soon again to know if the affair proceeds. I have mentioned it to none of my friends for fear of being laughed at for my disappointment.

[14] Johnson long kept vaguely secret his contribution of twenty-nine essays to *The Adventurer.*

[15] Warton and Wise were endeavoring to obtain for Johnson an Oxford M.A., so that he could write it after his name on the title-page of the Dictionary.

[16] The poet William Collins was losing his mind. "I have often been near his state, and therefore have it in great commiseration." (Letter to Joseph Warton, Dec. 24, 1754.)

You know poor Mr Dodsly has lost his Wife, I believe he is much affected. I hope he will not suffer so much as I yet suffer for the loss of mine.

Οἴμι· τι δ' οἴμι; θνῆτα γὰρ πεπόνθαμεν.[17]

I have ever since seemed to myself broken off from mankind a kind of solitary wanderer in the wild of life, without any certain direction, or fixed point of view. A gloomy gazer on a World to which I have little relation. Yet I would endeavour by the help of you and your brother to supply the want of closer union by friendship, and hope to have long the pleasure of being
Dear Sir
Most affectionately yours
Sam: Johnson

18. *To Thomas Warton, Oxford*

February 1, 1755
Dear Sir

. . . I now begin to see land, after having wandered, according to Mr Warburton's phrase, in this vast sea of words. What reception I shall meet with upon the Shore I know not, whether the sound of Bells and acclamations of the People which Ariosto talks of in his last canto or a general murmur of dislike, I know not whether I shall find upon the coast, a Calypso that will court or a Polypheme that will eat me.[18] But if Polypheme comes to me have at his eyes.

I hope however the criticks will let me be at peace for though I do not much fear their skill or strength, I am a little afraid of myself, and would not willingly feel so much ill-will in my bosom as literary quarrels are apt to excite. . . .

There is nothing considerable done or doing among us here, we

[17] "Alas—but why Alas? We have suffered the lot of man." (Euripides.)
[18] Calypso: the nymph who entertained the shipwrecked Odysseus for eight years; Polypheme: the Cyclops, who imprisoned Odysseus and ate his men until they put out his eye with a burning log.

are not perhaps as innocent as villagers but most of us seem to be as idle. I hope however you are busy, and should be glad to know what you are doing.

I am Dearest Sir,

Your most humble servant

Sam: Johnson

19. To the Earl of Chesterfield

February 7, 1755

My Lord

I have been lately informed by the proprietor of The World that two Papers in which my Dictionary is recommended to the Public were written by your Lordship. To be so distinguished is an honour which, being very little accustomed to favours from the Great, I know not well how to receive, or in what terms to acknowledge.

When upon some slight encouragment I first visited your Lordship I was overpowered like the rest of Mankind by the enchantment of your adress, and could not forbear to wish that I might boast myself Le Vainqueur du Vainqueur de la Terre,[19] that I might obtain that regard for which I saw the world contending, but I found my attendance so little incouraged, that neither pride nor modesty would suffer me to continue it. When I had once adressed your Lordship in public, I had exhausted all the art of pleasing which a retired and uncourtly Scholar can possess. I had done all that I could, and no Man is well pleased to have his all neglected, be it ever so little.

Seven years, My Lord, have now past since I waited in your outward Rooms or was repulsed from your Door, during which time I have been pushing on my work through difficulties of which It is useless to complain, and have brought it at last to the verge of Publication without one Act of assistance, one word of encouragement, or one smile of favour. Such treatment I did not expect, for I never had a Patron before.

The Shepherd in Virgil grew at last acquainted with Love, and found him a Native of the Rocks. Is not a Patron, My Lord, one

---

[19] "The conqueror of the conqueror of the world." (Boileau.)

who looks with unconcern on a Man struggling for Life in the water and when he has reached ground encumbers him with help. The notice which you have been pleased to take of my Labours, had it been early, had been kind; but it has been delayed till I am indifferent and cannot enjoy it, till I am solitary and cannot impart it, till I am known and do not want it.

I hope it is no very cinical asperity not to confess obligation where no benefit has been received, or to be unwilling that the Public should consider me as owing that to a Patron, which Providence has enabled me to do for myself.

Having carried on my work thus far with so little obligation to any Favourer of Learning I shall not be disappointed though I should conclude it, if less be possible, with less, for I have been long wakened from that Dream of hope, in which I once boasted myself with so much exultation,

My lord

Your Lordship's Most humble

Most Obedient Servant,

Sam: Johnson

1755-1759

On his honorary Oxford diploma, granted in March 1755, it was recorded (in Latin) that "the learned Samuel Johnson of Pembroke College has long been known to the world of letters by writings that have shaped the manners of his countrymen, and is even now laboring at a work of the greatest usefulness in adorning and fixing our native tongue." But M.A. or no M.A., Dictionary or no Dictionary, he still had to keep writing, and occasionally begging, "for money." For fifteen months he edited The Literary Magazine, contributing all sorts of political and literary reviews. He composed an obituary biography for Cave, and once again proposed his Shakespeare—an effort, recalling the Dictionary, that was to take him eight years longer than he anticipated. From 1758 to 1760 he composed his weekly Idler *essays, shorter, slightly more Addisonian versions of* The Rambler. *The range of his miscellaneous prefaces, dedications, and essays during these years defies the imagination. In March of 1759, hoping to reduce his expenses, he left the good house at Gough Square, and lived for the next six years in a series of rented rooms.*

The Dictionary had been finished at a particularly bleak moment. "I may surely be contented," he wrote at the end of its Preface, "without the praise of perfection, which if I could obtain in this gloom of solitude, what would it avail me? I have protracted my work till most of those whom I wished to please have sunk into the grave; and success and miscarriage are empty sounds. I therefore dismiss it with frigid tranquillity, having little to fear or hope from censure or from praise." This uncharacteristic whine—Johnson rarely complained so in public—may reveal nothing more than the deflation that any author feels at the end of so extended a chore. But part of its cause was radical, and the gloom was impressed still further by the death, in January of the following year, of dear Miss Boothby, a wise and good woman he may once have contemplated making the second Mrs. Johnson. The series of surviving letters to her is the closest to "love letters" we have from Johnson's hand, if love letters with a difference.

By 1758, despite these losses, and the continuing pressures of loneliness, poverty, and work, Johnson's temperament seems to have brightened. But the melancholy fit fell once more, in January of 1759, with the death of his mother at eighty-nine. He can scarcely be said to have loved her; he had not visited her for twenty-two years. But her death impressed him, as so many deaths were to do, with an awesome sense of guilt, of time, of duties undone. Idler 41, written a week after her death, and his letters to his stepdaughter Lucy bear eloquent testimony to his mood. Rasselas, his stiff, gloomy, profoundly wise "Eastern tale," was written in the evenings of one week, still in the shadow of her death, to pay the costs of his mother's funeral and "some little debts which she had left."

20. *To Thomas Warton, Oxford*

March 20, 1755

Dear Sir

After I received my diploma I wrote you a letter of thanks with a letter to the vice chancellor and sent another to Mr Wise, but have heard from nobody since, and begin to think myself forgotten. It is true I sent you a double letter, and you may fear an expensive correspondent,[1] but I would have taken it kindly if you had returned it treble, and what is a double letter to a *petty King* that having fellowship and fines can sleep without a modus in his head.[2]

Dear Mr Warton let me hear from you, and tell me something I care not what so I hear it but from you—Something I will tell you—I hope to see my Dictionary bound and lettered next week—vasta mole superbus,[3] and I have a great mind to come to Oxford at Easter, but you will not invite me, shall I come uninvited or stay here where nobody perhaps would miss me if I went. a hard choice but such is the world to

Dear Sir,

Your most humble servant

Sam: Johnson

21. *To Thomas Birch*

March 29, 1755

Sir

I have sent some parts of my dictionary such as were at hand for your Inspection. The favour which I beg is that if you do not like them you will say nothing.

I am, Sir,

Your most affectionate humble servt

Sam: Johnson

---

[1] Postage was paid by the recipient, and was relatively expensive.

[2] Johnson is quoting from a poem of Warton's. A modus is "something paid in compensation for tithes."

[3] "Proud in its huge bulk."

22. To Hill Boothby

December 30, 1755

Dear Madam

It is again Midnight, and I am again alone. With what meditation shall I amuse this waste hour of darkness and vacuity. If I turn my thoughts upon myself what do I perceive but a poor helpless being reduced by a blast of wind to weakness and misery. How my present distemper was brought upon me I can give no account, but impute it to some sudden succession of cold to heat, such as in the common road of life cannot be avoided, and against which no precaution can be taken.

Of the fallaciousness of hope, and the uncertainty of schemes every day gives some new proof, but it is seldom heeded till something rather felt than seen awakens attention. This Ilness in which I have suffered something and feared much more, has depressed my confidence and elation, and made me consider all that I have promised myself as less certain to be attained or enjoyed. I have endeavoured to form resolutions of a better life, but I form them weakly under the consciousness of an external motive. Not that I conceive a time of sickness a time improper for recollection and good purposes, which I believe Diseases and Calamities often sent to produce; but because no man can know how little his performance will answer to his promises, and designs are nothing in human eyes till they are realised by execution.

Continue, my Dearest, your prayers for me, that no good resolution may be vain. You think, I believe, better of me than I deserve. I hope to be in time what I wish to be, and what I have hitherto satisfied myself too readily with only wishing.

Your Billet brought me what I much wished to have, a proof that I am still remembered by you at the hour in which I most desire it!

The Doctor is anxious about you. He thinks you too negligent of yourself, if you will promise to be cautious, I will exchange promises, as we have already exchanged injunctions. However, do not write to me more than you can easily bear, do not interrupt your ease to write at all.

Mr Fitzherbert sent to day to offer me some Wine, the people about me say I ought to accept it, I shall therefore be obliged to him if he will send me a Bottle.

There has gone about a report that I died to day which I mention, lest you should hear it and be alarmed. You see that I think my death may alarm you, which for me is to think very highly of earthly friendship. I believe it arose from the death of one of my neighbours. You know Des Cartes's argument, 'I think therefore I am'. It is as good a consequence 'I write therefore I am alive'. I might give another 'I am alive therefore I love Miss Boothby'; but that I hope our friendship may be of far longer duration than life.

I am Dearest Madam with most sincere affection,

Your most obliged, and most humble servant

Sam: Johnson

23. *To Hill Boothby*

December 31, 1755

My Sweet Angel . . .

I sincerely hope that God whom you so much desire to serve aright will bless you, and restore you to health, if he sees it best. Surely no human understanding can pray for any thing temporal otherwise than conditionally. Dear Angel do not forget me. my heart is full of tenderness.

It has pleased God to permit me to be much better, which I believe will please you.

Give me leave, who have thought much on Medicine, to propose to you an easy and I think a very probable remedy for indigestion and lubricity of the bowels. Dr Laurence has told me your case. Take an ounce of dried orange peel finely powdered, divide it into scruples,[4] and take one Scruple at a time in any manner; the best way is perhaps to drink it in a glass of hot red port. or to eat it first and drink the wine after it. If you mix cinnamon or nutmeg with the powder it were not worse, but it will be more bulky and so more troublesome. This is a medicine not disgusting, not costly, easily tried, and if not found useful easily left off.

[4] An apothecary's measure, ⅓ dram. Johnson was "a great dabbler in physick." (Boswell.)

I would not have you offer it to the Doctor as mine. Physicians do not love intruders, yet do not take it without his leave. but do not be easily put off, for it is in my opinion very likely to help you, and not likely to do you harm, do not take too much in haste, a scruple one in three hours or about five scruples a day will be sufficient to begin, or less if you find any aversion. I think using sugar with it might be bad, if Syrup, use old Syrup of Quinces, but even that I do not like. I should think better of conserve of Sloes. Has the doctor mentioned the bark? [5] in powder you could hardly take it, perhaps you might bear the infusion?

Do not think me troublesome, I am full of care. I love you and honour you, and am very unwilling to lose you.

A Dieu Je vous commende.

I am Madam

Your most affectionate humble servant

Sam: Johnson.

My compliments to my dear Miss.

24. *To Hill Boothby*

January 1, 1756

Dearest Madam

Though I am afraid your ilness leaves you little leisure for the reception of airy civilities, yet I cannot forbear to pay you my congratulations on the new year, and to declare my Wishes, that your years to come may be many and happy. In this wish indeed I include myself who have none but you on whom my heart reposes, yet surely I wish your good even though your situation were such as should permit you to communicate no gratifications to

Dearest dearest Madam,

Your most obliged and most humble Servant

Sam: Johnson

[5] Quinine.

25. To Hill Boothby

Dearest Madam

Nobody but you can recompense me for the distress which I suffered on Monday night. Having engaged Dr Laurence to let me know, at whatever hour, the state in which he left you, I concluded when he staid so long, that he staid to see my dearest expire. I was composing myself as I could to hear what yet I hoped not to hear, when his Servant brought me word that you were better. Do you continue to grow better? let my dear little Miss inform me on a card. I would not have you write, lest it should hurt you, and consequently hurt likewise,

Dearest Madam,
Your most affectionate and faithful Servant
Sam: Johnson

26. To Hill Boothby

Honoured Madam

I beg of you to endeavour to live. I have returned your *Law*[6] which however I earnestly entreat you to give me. I am in great trouble, if you can write three words to me, be pleased to do it. I am afraid to say much, and cannot say nothing when my dearest is in danger.

The Allmercifull God have mercy on You.

I am Madam Your
Sam: Johnson[7]

---

[6] I.e., a devotional book of William Law's.
[7] Miss Boothby died on January 16.

27. *To Miss Elizabeth Carter*

January 14, 1756

Madam

From the liberty of writing to you if I have been hitherto detered by the fear of your understanding I am now encouraged to it by the confidence of your goodness.

I am soliciting a benefit for Miss Williams, and beg that if you can by letters influence any in her favour, and who is there whom you cannot influence? you will be pleased to patronise her on this occasion. You see the time is short and as you were not in town I did not till this day remember that you might help us, or recollect how widely and how rapidly light is diffused.

To every Joy is appended a Sorrow. The name of Miss Carter introduces the memory of Cave. Poor dear Cave I owed him much, for to him I owe that I have known you. He died, I am afraid, unexpectedly to himself, yet surely unburthened with any great crime, and for the positive duties of religion, I have yet no right to condemn him for neglect.

I am, with respect which I neither owe nor pay to any other
Madam,
Your most obedient and most humble Servant
Sam: Johnson

28. *To Samuel Richardson*

February 19, 1756

Dear Sir

I return you my sincerest thanks for the favour which you were pleased to do me two nights ago.

Be pleased to accept of this little book, which is all that I have published this winter. The inflammation is come again into my eye, so that I can read very little.

I am Sir
Your most obliged and most humble servant
Fryday   *Sam: Johnson*
(Endorsed by Richardson, "Mr. S. Johnson Arrested Tuesday 19 Febr. 1756")

29. To Samuel Richardson

March 16, 1756

Sir

I am obliged to entreat your assistance, I am now under an arrest for five pounds eighteen shillings. Mr Strahan from whom I should have received the necessary help in this case is not at home, and I am afraid of not finding Mr Millar, if you will be so good as to send me this sum, I will very gratfully repay You, and add it to all former obligations.

I am Sir,

Your most obedient and most humble Servant

Sam: Johnson

(Endorsed by Richardson, "March 16. 1756. Sent Six Guineas, Witness Wm Richardson")

30. To Edmund Hector, Birmingham

October 7, 1756

Dear Sir . . .

It is not in mere civility that I write now to you but to inform you that I have undertaken a new Edition of Shakespeare, and that the profits of it are to arise from a subscription, I therefore solicit the interest of all my friends, and believe myself sure of yours without solicitation. The proposals and receipts may be had from my Mother to whom I beg you to send for as many as you can dispose of, and to remit to her money which you or your acquaintance shall collect. Be so kind as to mention my undertaking to any other friends that I may have in your part of the kingdom, the activity of a few solicitors may produce great advantages to me.

I have been thinking every month of coming down into the country, but every month has brought its hinderances. From that kind of melancholy indisposition which I had when we lived together at Birmingham, I have never been free, but have always had it operating against my health and my life with more or less violence. I hope however to see all my friends, all that are remaining, in no very long time, and particularly you whom I always think on with great tenderness,

> I am, Sir,
> > Your most affectionate servant,
> > > *Sam: Johnson*

31. To Charles Burney, King's Lynn, Norfolk

> *December 24, 1757*

Sir

. . . I remember with great pleasure your commendation of my dictionary. Your praise was welcome not only because I believe it was sincere, but because praise has been very scarce. A man of your candour will be surprised when I tell you that among all my acquaintance there were only two who upon the publication of my book did not endeavour to depress me with threats of censure from the publick, or with objections learned from those who had learned them from my own preface. Yours is the only letter of good will that I have yet received, though indeed I am promised something of that sort from Sweden.

How my new Edition will be received I know not, the subscription has not been very successful. I shall publish about March.

If you can direct me how to send proposals I should wish that they were in such hands.

I remember, Sir, in some of the first letters with which you favoured me, you mentioned your Lady. May I enquire after her? In return for the favours which you have shewn me, it is not much to tell you that I wish you and her all that can conduce to your happiness.

> I am Sir
> > Your most obliged
> > > And most humble servant
> > > > *Sam: Johnson*

32. *To Jacob Tonson*

February 10, 1758

Sir

An accident has happened to me which Mr. Strahan will tell you, and from which I must try to be extricated by your assistance. The affair is about forty pounds. I think it necessary to assure you that no other such vexation can happen to me for I have no other of any consequence but to my friends.

I am Sir
Your most humble servant
Sam: Johnson

Feb. 10, 1758.

I promise to pay to Jacob Tonson, Esqr., the sum of Forty Pounds on demand.

£40 0 0   *Sam: Johnson*

33. *To Charles Burney, Lynne, Norfolk*

March 8, 1758

Sir . . .

I am ashamed to tell you that my Shakespeare will not be out so soon as I promised my subscribers; but I did not promise them more than I promised myself. It will however be published before summer.

I have sent you a bundle of proposals, which I think, do not profess more than I have hitherto performed. I have printed many of the plays and have hitherto left very few passages unexplained; where I am quite at a loss, I confess my ignorance, which is seldom done by commentators.

I have likewise enclosed twelve receipts, not that I mean to impose upon you the trouble of pushing them with more importunity than may seem proper, but that you may rather have more than fewer than you shall want. . . .

Since the Life of Brown I have been a little engaged, from time to time in the *Literary Magazine*, but not very lately. I have not the collection by me, and therefore cannot draw out a catalogue of my own parts, but will do it, and send it. Do not buy them, for I will

39

gather all those that have any thing of mine in them, and send them to Mrs. Burney, as a small token of gratitude for the regard which she is pleased to bestow upon me.

I am Sir
Your most obliged and most humble servant
Sam: Johnson

34. To Bennet Langton, Langton Near Spilsby, Lincolnshire

September 21, 1758

Dear Sir

I should be sorry to think that what engrosses the attention of my friend should have no part of mine. Your mind is now full of the fate of Dury, but his fate is past, and nothing remains but to try what reflection will suggest to mitigate the horrors of a violent death, which is more formidable at the first glance than on a nearer and more steady view. A violent death is never very painful, the only danger is lest it should be unprovided. But if a man can be supposed to make no provision for death in war, what can be the state that would have awakened him to the care of futurity; when would that man have prepared himself to die, who went to seek death without preparation?

What then can be the reason why we lament more him that dies of a wound than that dies of a fever? A Man that languishes with disease, ends his life with more pain, but with less virtue, he leaves no example to his friends, nor bequeaths any honour to his descendants.

The only reason why we lament a soldier's death is that we think he might have lived longer, yet this cause of grief is common to many other kinds of death which are not so passionately bewailed. The truth is that every death is violent which is the effect of accident, every death which is not gradually brought on by the miseries of age, or when life is extinguished for any other reason than that it is burnt out. He that dies before sixty, of a cold or consumption dies in reality, by a violent death; yet his end is borne with patience, only because the cause of his untimely end is silent and invisible. Let us endeavour to see things as they are, and then enquire whether we ought to complain. Whether to see life as it is will give us much consolation I know not, but the consolation which is drawn from truth, if any there be, is solid and durable, that which may be derived from errour must be like its original fallacious and fugitive.

I am Dear dear Sir
Your most humble Servant
Sam: Johnson

35. *To Bennet Langton, Langton*

January 9, 1759

Dearest Sir

I must have indeed slept very fast not to have been awakened by your letters. None of your suspicions are true, I am not much richer than when you left me, and what is worse, my omission of an answer to your first letter will prove that I am not much wiser. But I go on as I formerly did, designing to be some time or other both rich and wise, and yet cultivate neither mind nor fortune. Do you take notice of my example, and learn the danger of delay. When I was as You are now, towering in the confidence of twenty one, little did I suspect that I should be at forty nine what I now am. . . .

The two Wartons just looked into the town and were taken to see *Cleone* where David says they were starved for want of company to keep them warm. David and Doddy[8] have had a new quarrel, and I think cannot conveniently quarrel any more. Cleone was well acted by all the characters, but Bellamy left nothing to be desired. I went the first night and supported it, as publickly as I might; for Doddy, you know, is my patron, and I would not desert him. The play was very well received. Doddy after the danger was over went every night to the Stage side, and cried at the distress of poor Cleone.

I have left off housekeeping and therefore made presents of the game which you were pleased to send me. The Pheasant I gave to Mr Richardson, the Bustard to Dr. Lawrence, and the pot I placed

[8] David is David Garrick, "Doddy" the bookseller Robert Dodsley.

with Miss Williams, to be eaten by myself. She desires that her compliments, and good wishes may be accepted by the Family, and I make the same request for myself.

Mr Reynolds has within these few days raised his price to twenty Guineas a head, and Miss[9] is much employed in Miniatures. I know not any body else whose prosperity has encreased since you left them.

Murphy is to have his Orphan of China acted next month, and is therefore, I suppose, happy. I wish I could tell you of any great good to which I was approaching, but at present my prospects do not much delight me, however I am always pleased when I find that you, dear Sir, remember

Your affectionate humble servant
Sam: Johnson

36. To Sarah Johnson, Lichfield

January 13, 1759

Honoured Madam,

The account which Miss gives me of your health pierces my heart. God comfort and preserve you and save you, for the sake of Jesus Christ.

I would have Miss read to you from time to time the Passion of our Saviour, and sometimes the sentences in the Communion Service, beginning '*Come unto me, all ye that travel and are heavy laden, and I will give you rest*'.

I have just now read a physical book, which inclines me to think that a strong infusion of the bark would do you good. Do, dear mother, try it.

Pray, send me your blessing, and forgive all that I have done amiss to you. And whatever you would have done, and what debts you would have paid first, or anything else that you would direct, let Miss put it down; I shall endeavour to obey you.

I have got twelve guineas to send you, but unhappily am at a loss

[9] Frances Reynolds.

how to send it to-night. If I cannot send it to-night, it will come by the next post.

Pray, do not omit any thing mentioned in this letter: God bless you for ever and ever.

I am your dutiful son
Sam: Johnson

37. To Lucy Porter, Lichfield

January 16, 1759

My dear Miss,

I think myself obliged to you beyond all expression of gratitude for your care of my dear mother. God grant it may not be without success. Tell Kitty[10] that I shall never forget her tenderness for her mistress. Whatever you can do, continue to do. My heart is very full.

I hope you received twelve guineas on Monday. I found a way of sending them by means of the postmaster, after I had written my letter, and hope they came safe. I will send you more in a few days. God bless you all.

I am, my dear,
Your most obliged and most humble servant
Sam: Johnson

38. To Sarah Johnson, Lichfield

January 16, 1759

Dear honoured Mother

Your weakness afflicts me beyond what I am willing to communicate to you. I do not think you unfit to face death, but I know not how to bear the thought of losing you. Endeavour to do all you can for yourself. Eat as much as you can.

I pray often for you; do you pray for me. I have nothing to add to my last letter.

I am, dear, dear mother,
Your dutiful son,
Sam: Johnson

[10] Catherine Chambers.

39. To Sarah Johnson, Lichfield

January 18, 1759

Dear honoured Mother

I fear you are too ill for long letters; therefore I will only tell you, you have from me all the regard that can possible subsist in the heart. I pray God to bless you for evermore, for Jesus Christ's sake. Amen.

Let Miss write to me every post, however short.

I am, dear mother,
Your dutiful son
Sam: Johnson

40. To Lucy Porter, Lichfield

January 20, 1759

Dear Miss

I will, if it be possible, come down to you. God grant I may yet find my dear mother breathing and sensible. Do not tell her lest I disappoint her. If I miss to write next post, I am on the road.

I am, my dearest Miss,
Your most humble servant,
Sam: Johnson

41. To Sarah Johnson, Lichfield

January 20, 1759

Dear honoured Mother

Neither your condition nor your character make it fit for me to say much. You have been the best mother, and I believe the best woman in the world. I thank you for your indulgence to me, and beg forgiveness of all that I have done ill, and all that I have omitted to do well. God grant you his Holy Spirit, and receive you to everlasting happiness, for Jesus Christ's sake. Amen. Lord Jesus receive your spirit. Amen.

I am, dear, dear mother,
Your dutiful son,
Sam: Johnson

44

42. To William Strahan

January 20, 1759

Sir

When I was with you last night I told you of a thing which I was preparing for the press. The title will be

The choice of Life

or

The History of ————[11] Prince of Abissinia

It will make about two volumes like little Pompadour that is about one middling volume. The bargain which I made with Mr Johnston was seventy five pounds (or guineas) a volume, and twenty five pounds for the second Edition. I will sell this either at that price or for sixty the first edition of which he shall himself fix the number, and the property then to revert to me, or for forty pounds, and share the profit that is retain half the copy. I shall have occasion for thirty pounds on Monday night when I shall deliver the book which I must entreat you upon such delivery to procure me. I would have offered it to Mr Johnston, but have no doubt of selling it, on some of the terms mentioned.

I will not print my name, but expect it to be known.

I am Dear Sir

Your most humble Servant

Sam: Johnson

Get me the money if you can.

43. To Lucy Porter, Lichfield

January 23, 1759

You will conceive my sorrow for the loss of my mother, of the best mother. If she were to live again, surely I should behave better to her. But she is happy, and what is past is nothing to her; and for me, since I cannot repair my faults to her, I hope repentance will efface them. I return you and all those that have been good to her my sincerest thanks, and pray God to repay you all with infinite ad-

[11] *Rasselas.*

vantage. Write to me, and comfort me, dear child. I shall be glad likewise, if Kitty will write to me. I shall send a bill of twenty pounds in a few days, which I thought to have brought to my mother; but God suffered it not. I have not power or composure to say much more. God bless you and bless us all.

I am, dear Miss,
Your affectionate humble servant
Sam: Johnson

44. *To Lucy Porter, Lichfield*

May 10, 1759

Dear Madam

I am almost ashamed to tell you that all your letters came safe, and that I have been always very well, but hindered, I hardly know how, from writing. I sent, last week, some of my works, one for you, one for your aunt Hunter, who was with my poor dear mother when she died, one for Mr. Howard, and one for Kitty.

I beg you, my dear, to write often to me, and tell me how you like my little book.

I am, dear love,
Your affectionate humble servant
Sam: Johnson

45. *To Lucy Porter, Lichfield*

August 9, 1759

Dear Madam

I beg pardon for having been so long without writing. I have been for seven weeks at Oxford, and was very well used among them, but I have no great pleasure in any place. Please to let me know what money is necessary to pay what yet remains of my dear Mother's debts, for I expect to receive some in a short time. Be so kind as to write to me often though I should sometimes omit it, for I have no greater pleasure than to hear from you. My respects to Kitty.

I am My Dear
Your obliged humble Servant
Sam: Johnson

1760-1763

1760 brought young George III to the throne of England ("I cannot perhaps see another coronation so conveniently as this"), and George III brought financial independence to Samuel Johnson, with a generous pension in 1762. Whether or not the King knew what he was doing, the grant was a handsome sign of Johnson's recognition, after the publication of his Dictionary, as a figure of national importance, worthy of national patronage. Though he was careful to secure the Prime Minister's assurance that the bounty bore no political strings, he was not above turning out a few partisan pamphlets in subsequent years for "my friends at the ministry": little enough, he may have thought, for the freedom of three hundred pounds a year.

The relief thus provided served, at last, to reduce the constant pressure to write. Johnson could now write as he chose; he need no longer sing for his supper. He seems, in fact, to have done very little in these years except the usual prefaces and dedications. Shakespeare, *subscribers or no subscribers, seems almost to have been shelved entirely during the first years of Johnson's affluence.*

> *He for subscribers bates his hook,*
> *And takes their cash; but where's the book?*
> *No matter where; wise fear, we know,*
> *Forbids the robbing of a foe;*
> *But what, to serve our private ends,*
> *Forbids the cheating of our friends?*

The king's largesse, on the other hand, allowed Johnson a new leisure to expand, to begin to grow into the public character Boswell was soon to seek out and capture. He could now dedicate himself with a full, a gargantuan will to the great art of conversation, and begin to assume his new position as London's oracle-of-all-trades. He could now travel freely, to Lichfield, Devonshire, Oxford. Even his letters, as in the great series to Baretti, take on a new roundness, a personality, a relaxed expansiveness. Though he was not to earn the degree until 1765, the "Doctor Johnson" of popular legend was growing; and the co-maker of the legend, a young Scotsman of two-and-twenty, was on his way to London in November of 1762.

46. To Bennet Langton, Langton

October 18, 1760

Dear Sir,

You that travel about the world have more materials for letters than I who stay at home, and should therefore write with frequency proportionate to your opportunities. I should be glad to have all England surveyed by you, if you would impart your observations in narratives as agreeable as your last. Knowledge is always to be wished to those who can communicate it well. While you have been riding and running, and seeing the tombs of the learned, and the camps of the valiant, I have only staid at home, and intended to do great things which I have not done. Beau[1] went away to Cheshire,

[1] Topham Beauclerk.

and has not yet found his way back. Chambers passed the vacation at Oxford. . . .

Let me hear from you again, wherever you are, or whatever you are doing, whether you wander or sit still plant trees or make Rusticks, play with your Sisters, or muse alone; and in return I will tell you the success of Sheridan who at this instant is playing Cato, and has already played Richard twice.[2] He had more company the second than the first night, and will make I believe a good figure in the whole, though his faults seem to be very many, some of natural deficience, and some of laborious affectation. He has, I think no power of assuming either that Dignity or Elegance which some men who have little of either in common life, can exhibit on the stage. His voice when strained is unpleasing, and when low is not always heard. He seems to think too much on the audience, and turns his face too often to the Galleries.

However I wish him well, among other reasons because I like his wife.

Make haste to write to

Dear Sir,
Your most affectionate Servant
Sam: Johnson

47. *To Joseph Baretti, Milan*

June 10, 1761

You reproach me very often with parsimony of writing: but you may discover by the extent of my paper, that I design to recompense rarity by length. A short letter to a distant friend is, in my opinion, an insult like that of a slight bow or cursory salutation;—a proof of unwillingness to do much, even where there is a necessity of doing something. Yet it must be remembered, that he who continues the same course of life in the same place, will have little to tell. One week and one year are very like another. The silent changes made by time are not always perceived; and if they are not perceived, cannot be recounted. I have risen and lain down, talked and mused,

[2] In Addison's *Cato* and Shakespeare's *Richard II.* "Sheridan" is Thomas, the playwright's father.

while you have roved over a considerable part of Europe; yet I have not envied my Baretti any of his pleasures, though perhaps I have envied others his company; and I am glad to have other nations made acquainted with the character of the English, by a traveller who has so nicely inspected our manners, and so successfully studied our literature. I received your kind letter from Falmouth, in which you gave me notice of your departure for Lisbon; and another from Lisbon, in which you told me, that you were to leave Portugal in a few days. To either of these how could any answer be returned? I have had a third from Turin, complaining that I have not answered the former. Your English stile still continues in its purity and vigour. With vigour your genius will supply it; but its purity must be continued by close attention. To use two languages familiarly, and without contaminating one by the other, is very difficult; and to use more than two, is hardly to be hoped. The praises which some have received for their multiplicity of languages, may be sufficient to excite industry, but can hardly generate confidence.

I know not whether I can heartily rejoice at the kind reception which you have found, or at the popularity to which you are exalted. I am willing that your merit should be distinguished; but cannot wish that your affections may be gained. I would have you happy wherever you are; yet I would have you wish to return to England. If ever you visit us again, you will find the kindness of your friends undiminished. To tell you how many enquiries are made after you would be tedious or if not tedious, would be vain; because you may be told in a very few words, that all who knew you wish you well; and that all that you embraced at your departure, will caress you at your return: therefore do not let Italian academicians nor Italian ladies drive us from your thoughts. You may find among us what you will leave behind, soft smiles and easy sonnets. Yet I shall not wonder if all our invitations should be rejected: for there is a pleasure in being considerable at home, which is not easily resisted.

By conducting Mr. Southwell to Venice, you fulfilled, I know, the original contract: yet I would wish you not wholly to lose him from your notice, but to recommend him to such acquaintance as may best secure him from suffering by his own follies, and to take such general care both of his safety and his interest as may come within your power. His relations will thank you for any such gratuitous attention: at least they will not blame you for any evil that may happen, whether they thank you or not for any good.

You know that we have a new King and a new Parliament. Of the new Parliament Fitzherbert is a member. We were so weary of our old King, that we are much pleased with his successor; of whom we are so much inclined to hope great things, that most of us begin already to believe them. The young man is hitherto blameless; but it would be unreasonable to expect much from the immaturity of juvenile years, and the ignorance of princely education. He has been long in the hands of the Scots, and has already favoured them more than the English will contentedly endure. But perhaps he scarcely knows whom he has distinguished, or whom he has disgusted.[3]

The Artists have instituted a yearly exhibition of pictures and statues, in imitation, as I am told, of foreign Academies. This year was the second exhibition. They please themselves much with the multitude of spectators, and imagine that the English school will rise in reputation. Reynolds is without a rival, and continues to add thousands to thousands, which he deserves, among other excellencies, by retaining his kindness for Baretti. This exhibition has filled the heads of the Artists and lovers of art. Surely life, if it be not long, is tedious, since we are forced to call in the assistance of so many trifles to rid us of our time, of that time which never can return.

I know my Baretti will not be satisfied with a letter in which I give him no account of myself: yet what account shall I give him? I have not, since the day of our separation, suffered or done any thing considerable. The only change in my way of life is, that I have frequented the theatre more than in former seasons. But I have gone thither only to escape from myself. We have had many new farces, and the comedy called *The Jealous Wife*,[4] which, though not

---

[3] George III succeeded to the throne of his grandfather in 1760, at the age of 22. He was thought by many to be too much under the influence of his mother, the Princess Dowager, and her favorite, the Scottish Earl of Bute.

[4] By George Colman, the elder.

written with much genius, was yet so well adapted to the stage, and so well exhibited by the actors, that it was crowded for near twenty nights.[5] I am digressing from myself to the playhouse; but a barren plan must be filled with episodes. Of myself I have nothing to say, but that I have hitherto lived without the concurrence of my own judgment; yet I continue to flatter myself, that, when you return, you will find me mended. I do not wonder that, where the monastick life is permitted, every order finds votaries, and every monastery inhabitants. Men will submit to any rule, by which they may be exempted from the tyranny of caprice and of chance. They are glad to supply by external authority their own want of constancy and resolution, and court the government of others, when long experience has convinced them of their own inability to govern themselves. If I were to visit Italy, my curiosity would be more attracted by convents than by palaces; though I am afraid that I should find expectation in both places equally disappointed, and life in both places supported with impatience, and quitted with reluctance. That it must be so soon quitted, is a powerful remedy against impatience; but what shall free us from reluctance? Those who have endeavoured to teach us to die well, have taught few to die willingly; yet I cannot but hope that a good life might end at last in a contented death.

You see to what a train of thought I am drawn by the mention of myself. Let us now turn my attention upon you. I hope you take care to keep an exact journal, and to register all occurrences and observations; for your friends here expect such a book of travels as has not been often seen. You have given us good specimens in your letters from Lisbon. I wish you had staid longer in Spain, for no country is less known to the rest of Europe; but the quickness of your discernment must make amends for the celerity of your motions. He that knows which way to direct his view, sees much in a little time.

Write to me very often, and I will not neglect to write to you;

[5] Twenty nights was an exceptionally long run for the period. Johnson's *Irene* ran nine nights; Goldsmith's *She Stoops to Conquer* twelve.

and I may perhaps in time get something to write: at least, you will know by my letters, whatever else they may have or want, that I continue to be

Your most affectionate friend,
Samuel Johnson

48. To Thomas Percy, Easton Maudit, Northamptonshire

September 12, 1761

Dear Sir

The kindness of your invitation would tempt one to leave pomp and tumult behind, and hasten to your retreat, however as I cannot perhaps see another coronation so conveniently as this,[6] and I may see many young Percies, I beg your pardon for staying till this great ceremony is over after which I purpose to pass some time with you, though I cannot flatter myself that I can even then long enjoy the pleasure which your company always gives me, and which is likewise expected from that of Mrs Percy, by,

Sir,
Your most affectionate
Sam: Johnson

49. To George Staunton

June 1, 1762

Dear Sir

I make haste to answer your kind letter, in hope of hearing again from you before you leave us. I cannot but regret that a man of your qualifications should find it necessary to seek an establishment in Guadaloupe, which if a peace should restore to the French, I shall think it some alleviation of the loss, that it must restore likewise Dr. Staunton to the English.[7]

[6] George III was crowned on September 22, 1761.
[7] Guadeloupe, a valuable sugar island in the West Indies, was indeed restored to the French in 1763, as a part of the peace negotiations at the end of the Seven Years' War.

It is a melancholy consideration, that so much of our time is necessarily to be spent upon the care of living, and that we can seldom obtain ease in one respect but by resigning it in another; yet I suppose we are by this dispensation not less happy in the whole, than if the spontaneous bounty of Nature poured all that we want into our hands. A few, if they were thus left to themselves, would, perhaps, spend their time in laudable pursuits; but the greater part would prey upon the quiet of each other, or, in the want of other objects, would prey upon themselves.

This, however, is our condition, which we must improve and solace as we can: and though we cannot choose always our place of residence, we may in every place find rational amusements, and possess in every place the comforts of piety and a pure conscience.

In America there is little to be observed except natural curiosities. The new world must have many vegetables and animals with which philosophers are but little acquainted. I hope you will furnish yourself with some books of natural history, and some glasses and other instruments of observation. Trust as little as you can to report; examine all you can by your own senses. I do not doubt but you will be able to add much to knowledge, and, perhaps, to medicine. Wild nations trust to simples; and, perhaps, the Peruvian bark is not the only specifick which those extensive regions may afford us.[8]

Wherever you are, and whatever be your fortune, be certain, dear Sir, that you carry with you my kind wishes; and that whether you return hither, or stay in the other hemisphere, to hear that you are happy will give pleasure to,

Sir,

Your most affectionate humble servant.

Sam: Johnson.

---

[8] Simple, "a single ingredient in a medicine; a drug"; Specifick, "[In medicine] Appropriated to the cure of some particular distemper." (Johnson's Dictionary.) The Peruvian bark is cinchona, the source of quinine.

50. *To A Lady*

Madam

I hope you will believe that my delay in answering Your letter could proceed only from my unwillingness to destroy any hope that You had form'd. Hope is itself a species of happiness, & perhaps the chief happiness which this World affords, but like all other pleasures immoderately enjoyed, the excesses of hope must be expiated by pain, & expectations improperly indulged must end in disappointment. If it be asked, what is the improper expectation which it is dangerous to indulge, experience will quickly answer, that it is such expectation, dictated not by reason but by desire; expectation raised not by the common occurrences of life but by the wants of the Expectant; an Expectation that requires the common course of things to be changed, and the general rules of Action to be broken.

When you made Your request to me, You should have considered, Madam, what You were asking. You ask me to solicit a great Man to whom I never spoke, for a young Person whom I had never seen, upon a supposition which I had no means of knowing to be true. There is no reason why amongst all the great, I should chuse to supplicate the Archbishop, nor why among all the possible objects of his bounty, the Archbishop should chuse your Son. I know, Madam, how unwillingly conviction is admitted, when interest opposes it; but surely, Madam, You must allow that there is no reason why that should be done by me which every other man may do with equal reason, and which indeed no man can do properly without some very particular Relation both to the Archbishop & to You. If I could help You in this exigence by any proper means, it would give me pleasure, but this proposal is so very remote from all usual methods, that I cannot comply with it, but at the risque of such answer & suspicions, as I believe you do not wish me to undergo.

I have seen your Son this morning, he seems a pretty Youth, and will perhaps find some better friend than I can procure him, but though he should at last miss the University he may still be wise, useful, & happy.

I am Madam,
Your most humble Servant,
Sam: Johnson

51. To Joseph Baretti, Milan

July 20, 1762

Sir

However justly you may accuse me for want of punctuality in correspondence, I am not so far lost in negligence, as to omit the opportunity of writing to you, which Mr. Beauclerk's passage through Milan affords me.

I suppose you received the Idlers, and I intend that you shall soon receive Shakespeare, that you may explain his works to the ladies of Italy, and tell them the story of the editor, among the other strange narratives with which your long residence in this unknown region has supplied you.

As you have now been long away, I suppose your curiosity may pant for some news of your old friends. Miss Williams and I live much as we did. Miss Cotterel still continues to cling to Mrs. Porter, and Charlotte is now big of the fourth child. Mr. Reynolds gets six thousand a year. Levet is lately married, not without much suspicion that he has been wretchedly cheated in his match.[9] Mr. Chambers is gone this day, for the first time, the circuit with the Judges. Mr. Richardson is dead of an apoplexy, and his second daughter has married a merchant.

My vanity, or my kindness, makes me flatter myself, that you would rather hear of me than of those whom I have mentioned; but of myself I have very little which I care to tell. Last winter I went down to my native town, where I found the streets much narrower and shorter than I thought I had left them, inhabited by a new race of people, to whom I was very little known. My play-fellows were grown old, and forced me to suspect, that I was no longer young. My only remaining friend has changed his principles, and was become the tool of the predominant faction. My daughter-in-law,[10] from whom I expected most, and whom I met with sincere benevolence, has lost the beauty and gaiety of youth, without having gained much of the wisdom of age. I wandered about for five days,

---

[9] Johnson's poor lodger Levett had married a streetwalker, who, learning of his poverty, left him in short order.
[10] Lucy Porter.

and took the first convenient opportunity of returning to a place, where, if there is not much happiness, there is at least such a diversity of good and evil, that slight vexations do not fix upon the heart.

I think in a few weeks to try another excursion; though to what end? Let me know, my Baretti, what has been the result of your return to your own country: whether time has made any alteration for the better, and whether, when the first raptures of salutation were over, you did not find your thoughts confessed their disappointment.

Moral sentences appear ostentatious and tumid, when they have no greater occasions than the journey of a wit to his own town: yet such pleasures and such pains make up the general mass of life; and as nothing is little to him that feels it with great sensibility, a mind able to see common incidents in their real state, is disposed by very common incidents to very serious contemplations. Let us trust that a time will come, when the present moment shall be no longer irksome; when we shall not borrow all our happiness from hope, which at last is to end in disappointment.

I beg that you will shew Mr. Beauclerk all the civilities which you have in your power; for he has always been kind to me.

I have lately seen Mr. Stratico, Professor of Padua, who has told me of your quarrel with an Abbot of the Celestine Order; but had not the particulars very ready in his memory. When you write to Mr. Marsili, let him know that I remember him with kindness.

May you, my Baretti, be very happy at Milan, or some other place nearer to,

Sir,
Your most affectionate humble servant,
Sam: Johnson

52. *To the Earl of Bute*

July 20, 1762

My Lord

When the bills were yesterday delivered to me by Mr. Wedderburne, I was informed by him of the future favours which his

Majesty has, by your Lordship's recommendation, been induced to intend for me.

Bounty always receives part of its value from the manner in which it is bestowed; your Lordship's kindness includes every circumstance that can gratify delicacy, or enforce obligation. You have conferred your favours on a man who has neither alliance nor interest, who has not merited them by services, nor courted them by officiousness; you have spared him the shame of solicitation, and the anxiety of suspense.

What has been thus elegantly given, will, I hope, not be reproachfully enjoyed; I shall endeavour to give your Lordship the only recompense which generosity desires,—the gratification of finding that your benefits are not improperly bestowed. I am, my Lord,
Your Lordship's most obliged, most obedient,
and most humble Servant,
Sam: Johnson

53. *To Lucy Porter, Lichfield*

July 24, 1762

Dear Madam

If I write but seldom to you, it is because it seldom happens that I have any thing to tell you that can give you pleasure, but last Monday I was sent for by the chief Minister the Earl of Bute, who told me that the King had empowered him to do something for me, and let me know that a pension was granted me of three hundred a year. Be so kind as to tell Kitty.
I am Dearest Madam
Your most affectionate
Sam: Johnson

54. *To the Earl of Bute*

November 3, 1762

My Lord

That generosity by which I was recommended to the favour of his Majesty, will not be offended at a solicitation necessary to make that favour permanent and effectual.

The pension appointed to be paid me at Michaelmas I have not received, and know not where or from whom I am to ask it. I beg therefore that your Lordship will be pleased to supply Mr. Wedderburne with such directions as may be necessary, which I believe his friendship will make him think it no trouble to convey to me.

To interrupt your Lordship at a time like this with such petty difficulties is improper and unseasonable, but your knowledge of the world has long since taught you, that every man's affairs, however little, are important to himself. Every Man hopes that he shall escape neglect, and with reason may every man, whose vices do not preclude his claim, expect favour from that beneficence which has been extended to

My Lord
  Your Lordship's most obliged and most humble Servant
              Sam: Johnson

55. To Joseph Baretti, Milan

December 21, 1762

Sir

You are not to suppose, with all your conviction of my idleness, that I have passed all this time without writing to my Baretti. I gave a letter to Mr. Beauclerk, who, in my opinion, and in his own, was hastening to Naples for the recovery of his health; but he has stopped at Paris, and I know not when he will proceed. Langton is with him.

I will not trouble you with speculations about peace and war. The good or ill success of battles and embassies extends itself to a very small part of domestic life: we all have good and evil, which we feel more sensibly than our petty part of public miscarriage or prosperity. I am sorry for your disappointment, with which you seem more touched than I should expect a man of your resolution and experience to have been, did I not know that general truths are seldom applied to particular occasions; and that the fallacy of our self-love extends itself as wide as our interest or affections. Every man believes that mistresses are unfaithful, and patrons capricious; but he excepts his own mistress and his own patron. We have all learned that greatness is negligent and contemptuous, and that in Courts life is often languished away in ungratified expectation; but he that approaches greatness, or glitters in a Court, imagines that destiny has at last exempted him from the common lot.

Do not let such evils overwhelm you as thousands have suffered and thousands have surmounted; but turn your thoughts with vigour to some other plan of life, and keep always in your mind, that, with due submission to Providence, a man of genius has been seldom ruined but by himself. Your patron's weakness or insensibility will finally do you little hurt, if he is not assisted by your own passions. Of your love I know not the propriety, nor can estimate the power; but in love, as in every other passion, of which hope is the essence, we ought always to remember the uncertainty of events. There is indeed nothing that so much seduces reason from her vigilance, as the thought of passing life with an amiable woman; and if all would happen that a lover fancies, I know not what other terrestrial happiness would deserve pursuit. But love and marriage are different states. Those who are to suffer the evils together, and to suffer often for the sake of one another, soon lose that tenderness of look and that benevolence of mind which arose from the participation of unmingled pleasure and successive amusement. A woman we are sure will not be always fair; we are not sure she will always be virtuous: and man cannot retain through life that respect and assiduity by which he pleases for a day or for a month. I do not however pretend to have discovered that life has any thing more to be desired than a prudent and virtuous marriage; therefore know not what counsel to give you.

If you can quit your imagination of love and greatness, and leave your hopes of preferment and bridal raptures to try once more the fortune of literature and industry, the way through France is now open.[11] We flatter ourselves that we shall cultivate with great diligence the arts of peace; and every man will be welcome among us who can teach us any thing we do not know. For your part, you will find all your old friends willing to receive you.

Reynolds still continues to encrease in reputation and in riches.

[11] The Seven Years' War with France ended formally on February 10, 1763.

Miss Williams, who very much loves you, goes on in the old way. Miss Cotterel is still with Mrs. Porter. Miss Charlotte is married to Dean Lewis, and has three children. Mr. Levet has married a street-walker. But the gazette of my narration must now arrive to tell you, that Bathurst went physician to the army, and died at the Havannah.[12]

I know not whether I have not sent you word that Huggins and Richardson are both dead. When we see our enemies and friends gliding away before us, let us not forget that we are subject to the general law of mortality, and shall soon be where our doom will be fixed for ever.

I pray God to bless you, and am,

> Sir,
> Your most affectionate humble servant,

Write soon.   *Sam: Johnson*

56. To George Grenville

July 2, 1763

Sir

Be pleased to pay to the bearer seventy-five pounds, being the quarterly payment of a pension granted by His Majesty, and due on the 24th day of June last to

> Sir,
> Your most humble Servant,
> *Sam: Johnson.*

---

[12] The expedition against Spanish Cuba in October 1762.

1763-1773

It was on May 16, 1763, in a bookseller's shop off Covent Garden, that James Boswell first met Samuel Johnson. From that moment he deliberately cultivated the acquaintance, as he was to cultivate the acquaintance of many great men. Boswell records the conversations of seventeen encounters that summer, and it is in these pages of his Life of Johnson that the strongest talker of English history first looms so hugely into life. By the time Boswell sailed for Holland from Harwich in August for his famous Grand Tour, he had so attached himself to Johnson that the latter accompanied him to the port to see him off.

For us, his friendship with Boswell is the most important Johnson ever formed; for him it was less consequential. After the first summer, Boswell, intent on his own continental affairs, was not to see

Johnson again for two and a half years. His visits during these ten years, in fact, from their first meeting to their tour of the Hebrides, were confined to a few busy weeks of talk each spring in 1766, '68, '72, and '73, and the fall of 1769, when Boswell came down to London from Scotland. The relationship, however, was genuine, intimate, and decidedly productive. If the early letters betray a certain studied, avuncular distance, they later grow more friendly and free.

Far more important for Johnson was his meeting, early in 1765, with the Thrales. The wealthy brewer and his wife were to provide Johnson with all the comforts of a home, a family, and a ready audience for almost twenty years, to take him with them to France, to Wales, and, almost, to Italy. Their "adoption" did even more than the king's pension had done to exempt him, as far as exemption was possible, from the "solicitudes of life." The puzzling, lively Mrs. Thrale was to become his prime correspondent: 369 of his surviving letters are to her. He vacationed with them in Brighton in 1765 and 1769, spent three months at their Streatham villa outside London in 1766, and in every year had his apartment always ready at each of their fine homes.

Understandably, perhaps, he did little work in this decade: "I am not obliged to do any more." He managed to bring forth the long-gestating Shakespeare *in 1765. He revised his Dictionary, wrote two sharp political pamphlets (these were the troubled years of John Wilkes and the first "democratic" demonstrations); he helped Hamilton with his speeches and Chambers with his law lectures; he turned out a few prologues and prefaces. But all this took a very small part of his time: the rest was filled with talk. Honors piled on his head: the Dublin LL.D., the conversation with George III. He formed, with the other great men of the Age of Johnson—Burke, Reynolds, Goldsmith—"The Club," the great weekly conversation society that was later to absorb most of the illuminati of the half-century. Dr. Maxwell, a reverend friend, has described a typical day:*

> *His general mode of life, during my acquaintance, seemed to be pretty uniform. About twelve o'clock I commonly visited him, and frequently found him in bed, or declaiming over his tea, which he*

drank very plentifully. He generally had a levee of morning visitors, chiefly men of letters; Hawkesworth, Goldsmith, Murphy, Langton, Steevens, Beauclerk, &c. &c. and sometimes learned ladies; particularly I remember a French lady of wit and fashion doing him the honour of a visit. He seemed to me to be considered as a kind of publick oracle, whom every body thought they had a right to visit and consult; and doubtless they were well rewarded. I never could discover how he found time for his compositions. He declaimed all the morning, then went to dinner at a tavern, where he commonly staid late, and then drank his tea at some friend's house, over which he loitered a great while, but seldom took supper. I fancy he must have read and wrote chiefly in the night, for I can scarcely recollect that he ever refused going with me to a tavern, and he often went to Ranelagh, which he deemed a place of innocent recreation.

These letters, however, reveal not so much the London-loving Monarch of Good Talk, the dominating Public Johnson—for this we must look to Boswell—as a Johnson more personal, more softened and pained, less assured. Most often he is writing home to London from some quiet country setting. He visited Langton and Percy in 1764, went to Cambridge in 1765, to Oxford many times. He spent six months at Lichfield in 1767, was back again each year from 1769 to 1772. The "ramble through the Midlands"—Lichfield, Ashbourne, sometimes Birmingham and Oxford—was to become something of an annual event.

These were not healthy years, for all the talk and travel. A deep melancholia, a neurotic despair reminiscent of 1729 and 1759, overcame him in 1765 and dragged on through the decade—perhaps in part a result of his liberation from the discipline of work. The gloom sunk deepest through 1768 and 1769: "I would consent to have a limb amputated to recover my spirits." He was physically as well as mentally oppressed, and a severe attack of rheumatism in 1770 left him sleepless and in pain for yet another year. The work of revising the Dictionary helped a bit to clear his haunted head, but a racking cough and fever beset him in 1773, and an inflammation of his one good eye brought him near to blindness on the eve of the Northern tour. The strange French letter to Mrs. Thrale is evidence —evidence corroborated by other letters and by the pleading, *desperate diaries—that he had had himself kept under lock and key at times for fear of going mad. This is the Johnson we must fit somehow against Boswell's, if we are to understand these extraordinary years. "It is not a very happy state," he wrote Taylor in 1773, "when the mere preservation of life, becomes its chief business."*

57. To James Boswell, Utrecht, Holland

December 8, 1763

Dear Sir

You are not to think yourself forgotten, or criminally neglected, that you have had yet no letter from me. I love to see my friends, to hear from them, to talk to them, and to talk of them; but it is not without a considerable effort of resolution that I prevail upon myself to write. I would not, however, gratify my own indolence by the omission of any important duty, or any office of real kindness.

To tell you that I am or am not well, that I have or have not been in the country, that I drank your health in the room in which we sat last together, and that your acquaintance continue to speak of you with their former kindness, topicks with which those letters are commonly filled which are written only for the sake of writing, I seldom shall think worth communicating; but if I can have it in my power to calm any harassing disquiet, to excite any virtuous desire, to rectify any important opinion, or fortify any generous resolution, you need not doubt but I shall at least wish to prefer the pleasure of gratifying a friend much less esteemed than yourself, before the gloomy calm of idle vacancy. Whether I shall easily arrive at an exact punctuality of correspondence, I cannot tell. I shall, at present, expect that you will receive this in return for two which I have had from you. The first, indeed, gave me an account so hopeless of the state of your mind, that it hardly admitted or deserved an answer; by the second I was much better pleased; and the pleasure will still be increased by such a narrative of the progress of your studies, as may evince the continuance of an equal and rational application of your mind to some useful enquiry.

You will, perhaps, wish to ask, what study I would recommend.

I shall not speak of theology, because it ought not to be considered as a question whether you shall endeavour to know the will of God. I shall, therefore, consider only such studies as we are at liberty to pursue or to neglect; and of these I know not how you will make a better choice, than by studying the civil law, as your father advises, and the ancient languages, as you had determined for yourself; at least resolve, while you remain in any settled residence, to spend a certain number of hours every day amongst your books. The dissipation of thought, of which you complain, is nothing more than the vacillation of a mind suspended between different motives, and changing its direction as any motive gains or loses strength. If you can but kindle in your mind any strong desire, if you can but keep predominant any wish for some particular excellence or attainment, the gusts of imagination will break away, without any effect upon your conduct, and commonly without any traces left upon the memory.

There lurks, perhaps, in every human heart a desire of distinction, which inclines every man first to hope, and then to believe, that Nature has given him something peculiar to himself. This vanity makes one mind nurse aversions, and another actuate desires, till they rise by art much above their original state of power; and as affectation, in time, improves to habit, they at last tyrannise over him who at first encouraged them only for show. Every desire is a viper in the bosom, who, while he was chill, was harmless; but when warmth gave him strength, exerted it in poison. You know a gentleman,[1] who, when first he set his foot in the gay world, as he prepared himself to whirl in the vortex of pleasure, imagined a total indifference and universal negligence to be the most agreeable concomitants of youth, and the strongest indication of an airy temper and a quick apprehension. Vacant to every object, and sensible of every impulse, he thought that all appearance of diligence would deduct something from the reputation of genius; and hoped that he should appear to attain, amidst all the ease of carelessness and all the tumult of diversion, that knowledge and those accomplishments which mortals of the common fabrick obtain only by mute

---

[1] The gentleman is Boswell.

abstraction and solitary drudgery. He tried this scheme of life awhile, was made weary of it by his sense and his virtue, he then wished to return to his studies; and finding long habits of idleness and pleasure harder to be cured than he expected, still willing to retain his claim to some extraordinary prerogatives, resolved the common consequences of irregularity into an unalterable decree of destiny, and concluded that Nature had originally formed him incapable of rational employment.

Let all such fancies, illusive and destructive, be banished henceforward from your thoughts for ever. Resolve, and keep your resolution; choose, and pursue your choice. If you spend this day in study, you will find yourself still more able to study to-morrow; not that you are to expect that you shall at once obtain a complete victory. Depravity is not very easily overcome. Resolution will sometimes relax, and diligence will sometimes be interrupted; but let no accidental surprize or deviation, whether short or long, dispose you to despondency. Consider these failings as incident to all mankind. Begin again where you left off, and endeavour to avoid the seducements that prevailed over you before.

This, my dear Boswell, is advice which, perhaps, has been often given you, and given you without effect. But this advice, if you will not take from others, you must take from your own reflections, if you purpose to do the duties of the station to which the bounty of Providence has called you.

Let me have a long letter from you as soon as you can. I hope you continue your journal, and enrich it with many observations upon the country in which you reside. It will be a favour if you can get me any books in the Frisick language, and can enquire how the poor are maintained in the Seven Provinces.[2]

I am, dear Sir,

Your most affectionate servant,

Sam: Johnson

---

[2] "Frisick" is Frisian, an ancient low-German dialect related to Anglo-Saxon. The Seven Provinces are the Netherlands.

58. To David Garrick

May 18, 1765

Dear Sir

I know that great regard will be had to your opinion of an Edition of Shakespeare. I desire therefore to secure an honest prejudice in my favour by securing your suffrage, and that this prejudice may really be honest, I wish you would name such plays as you would see, and they shall be sent you by

Sir

Your most humble servant

Sam: Johnson

59. To John Taylor, Ashbourne

July 15, 1765

Dear Sir

It is so long since I heard from you that I know not well whither to write. With all your building and feasting you might have found an hour in some wet day for the remembrance of your old friend. I should have thought that since you have led a life so festive and gay, you would have invited me to partake of your hospitality. I do not know but I may come invited or uninvited, and pass a few days with you in august or september, unless you send me a prohibition, or let me know that I shall be insupportably burthensome. Let me know your thoughts on this matter, because I design to go some place or other, and would be loth to produce any inconvenience for my own gratification.

Let me know how you go on in the world, and what entertainment may be expected in your new room by,

Dear Sir

Your most affectionate Servant

Sam: Johnson

60. To Mrs. Thrale, Brighthelmston[3]

August 13, 1765

Madam

If you have really so good an opinion of me as you express, it will not be necessary to inform you how unwillingly I miss the opportunity of coming to Brighthelmston in Mr. Thrale's company, or since I cannot do what I wish first, how eagerly I shall catch the second degree of pleasure by coming to you and Him, as soon as I can dismiss my work from my hands.

I am afraid to make promises even to myself, but I hope that the week after the next, will be the end of my present business. When business is done what remains but pleasure? and where should pleasure be sought but under Mrs Thrale's influence?

Do not blame me for a delay by which I must suffer so much, and by which I suffer alone. If you cannot think I am good, pray think I am mending, and that in time I may deserve to be,

> Dear Madam,
> Your most obedient and most humble servant
> *Sam: Johnson*

61. To Joseph Warton, Winchester

October 9, 1765

Dear Sir, . . .

I have taken care of your book;[4] being so far from doubting your subscription, that I think you have subscrib'd twice: you once paid your guinea into my own hand in the garret in Gough Square. When you light on your receipt, throw it on the fire; if you find a second receipt, you may have a second book.

To tell the truth, as I felt no solicitude about this work, I receive

[3] Brighton.
[4] His copy of Johnson's *Shakespeare.*

no great comfort from its conclusion; but yet am well enough pleased that the public has no further claim upon me. I wish you would write more frequently to,

Dear Sir,

Your affectionate humble servant,

Sam. Johnson.

62. *To Thomas Leland*

October 17, 1765

Sir,

Among the names subscribed to the degree which I have had the honour of receiving from the University of Dublin, I find none of which I have any personal knowledge but those of Doct^r Andrews & yourself.

Men are to be estimated by those who know them not, only as they are represented by those who know them, & therefore I flatter myself that I owe much of the pleasure which this distinction gives me, to your concurrence with Dr. Andrews in recommending me to the learned Society.

Having desired the Provost to return my general thanks to the University, I beg that you, Sir, will accept my particular and immediate acknowledgements.

I am, Sir,

Your most obedient and most humble Servant

Sam: Johnson

63. *To Jacob Tonson*

October 19, 1765

Sir

I have lately heard, and heard so often that I can hardly any longer refuse credit, that my Edition⁵ is sold stiched by the Booksellers (I am afraid at your own Shop) for Forty Shillings that is for four shillings under the Subscription. The Subscription was set-

---

⁵ Of Shakespeare.

tled with your consent; and your consent alone implied a promise that you would not undersel me. This promise was likewise verbally made by you in my room in Gough Square, when we treated about the Edition. This is the worse, as the demand for the Book has been such, as left [you] no temptation to lower the price.

If your Servants have acted without orders, it is time that some direction should be given. If it be done with your knowledge, it is an action which I have a right to resent. But I would willingly think it negligence or mistake.

> I am Sir your most humble Servant
> *Sam: Johnson*

64. To James Boswell, Paris

January 14, 1766

Dear Sir

. . . when you return, you will return to an unaltered, and, I hope, unalterable friend.

All that you have to fear from me is the vexation of disappointing me. No man loves to frustrate expectations which have been formed in his favour; and the pleasure which I promise myself from your journals and remarks is so great, that perhaps no degree of attention or discernment will be sufficient to afford it.

Come home, however, and take your chance. I long to see you, and to hear you; and hope that we shall not be so long separated again. Come home, and expect such a welcome as is due to him, whom a wise and noble curiosity has led, where perhaps no native of this country ever was before. . . .[6]

---

[6] These affectionate lines were quoted by Boswell in his *Account of Corsica* (1768), which drew down the wrath of Johnson's Letter 70.

65. *To Bennet Langton, Langton near Spilsby, Lincolnshire*

March 8, 1766

Dear Sir, . . .

Since you will not inform us where you are, or how you live, I know not whether you desire to know any thing of us. However I will tell you that the Club subsists, but we have less of Burke's company since he has been engaged in publick business, in which he has gained more reputation than perhaps any man at his appearance ever gained before. He made two speeches in the house for repealing the Stamp-act, which were publickly commended by Mr. Pit, and have filled the town with wonder.

Burke is a great man by Nature, and is expected soon to attain civil greatness. I am grown greater too, for I have maintained the newspapers these many weeks, and what is greater still, I have risen every morning since Newyears day at about eight, when I was up, I have indeed done but little, yet it is no slight advancement to obtain for so many hours more the consciousness of being.[7]

I wish you were in my new study, I am now writing the first letter in it. I think it looks very pretty about me.

Dyer is constant at the Club, Hawkins is remiss. I am not over diligent. Dr. Nugent, Dr. Goldsmith, and Mr. Reynolds are very constant. Mr. Lye is printing his Saxon and Gothick dictionary; all the Club subscribes.

You will pay my compliments to all my Lincolnshire friends.

I am, dear Sir,

Most affectionately your's,

Sam: Johnson

[7] "To rise early" was one of Johnson's vain resolutions in every New Year's prayer. The first six months of 1766 were the only recorded period of his adult life when he was consistently up before midday.

66. *To James Boswell, Edinburgh*

August 21, 1766

Dear Sir,

. . . Your resolution to obey your father I sincerely approve; but do not accustom yourself to enchain your volatility by vows: they will sometime leave a thorn in your mind, which you will, perhaps, never be able to extract or eject. Take this warning, it is of great importance.

The study of the law is what you very justly term it, copious and generous; and in adding your name to its professors, you have done exactly what I always wished, when I wished you best. I hope that you will continue to pursue it vigorously and constantly. You gain, at least, what is no small advantage, security from those troublesome and wearisome discontents, which are always obtruding themselves upon a mind vacant, unemployed, and undetermined.

You ought to think it no small inducement to diligence and perseverance, that they will please your father. We all live upon the hope of pleasing somebody; and the pleasure of pleasing ought to be greatest, and at last always will be greatest, when our endeavours are exerted in consequence of our duty.

Life is not long, and too much of it must not pass in idle deliberation how it shall be spent; deliberation, which those who begin it by prudence, and continue it with subtilty, must, after long expence of thought, conclude by chance. To prefer one future mode of life to another, upon just reasons, requires faculties which it has not pleased our Creator to give us.

If, therefore, the profession you have chosen has some unexpected inconveniencies, console yourself by reflecting that no profession is without them; and that all the importunities and perplexities of business are softness and luxury, compared with the incessant cravings of vacancy, and the unsatisfactory expedients of idleness.

> *Haec sunt quae nostrâ potui te voce monere;*
> *Vade, age.*[8]

As to your History of Corsica, you have no materials which others

[8] "Of these things may you be admonished by our voice. Come now, proceed." (Virgil.)

have not, or may not have. You have, somehow or other, warmed your imagination. I wish there were some cure, like the lover's leap, for all heads of which some single idea has obtained an unreasonable and irregular possession. Mind your own affairs, and leave the Corsicans to theirs.[9]

I am, dear Sir,

Your most humble servant,

Sam: Johnson.

67. To Sir James Caldwell

February 12, 1767

Dear Sir James

Our friend Doctor Hawkesworth acquaints me that you are very desirous to see a paper reciting a conversation with which his Majesty was pleased to honour me last Tuesday in his library. The moment I left the King's presence I put it down in writing as nearly as I could recollect, and send you a copy of it enclosed.

The King's information of what is going on in the literary as well as political world is much more extensive than is generally imagined.

I have read with pleasure what you have wrote to honest George[10] in favour of poor Mrs. Williams's subscription, and shall return it to you with a little emendation. You have taken the hints I gave you and illucidated and enforced them with great ability. You know I never flatter.

I am, my dear Sir, affectionately yours

Samuel Johnson

Don't forget the party we made to dine at the Mitre next Tuesday. I have engaged Hool, the translator of Tasso to be with us. Do not engage yourself, and you and I will drink tea with Mrs. Williams, and regale her with your letter to Faulkner. I am in bed, and I got

[9] Boswell had warmly attached himself to the cause of Corsican independence, as the little island was juggled back and forth between Genoa and France. His *Account of Corsica* was his most famous publication before the *Life of Johnson*.

[10] George Faulkner. Anna Williams, Johnson's blind housemate, was undertaking to have her *Miscellanies* published by subscription.

Davis to write this.[11] I hope it will overtake you before you go to Bromley.

68. To Robert Chambers, Oxford

Lichfield, 1767

Dear Sir . . .

I have passed this summer very uneasily. My old melancholy has laid hold upon me to a degree sometimes not easily supportable. God has been pleased to grant me some remission for a few days past. . . .

69. To Richard Penneck

Oxford, March 3, 1768

Sir

I am flattered by others with an honour with which I dare not presume to flatter myself, that of having gained so much of your kindness or regard, as that my recommendation of a Candidate for Southwark, may have some influence in determining your vote at the approaching election. As a Man is willing to believe well of himself I now indulge my Vanity by soliciting your Vote and Interest for MR THRALE, whose encomium I shall make very compendiously by telling you, that you would most certainly vote for him if you knew him. I ought to have waited on you with this request, even though my right to make it, had been greater. But as the Election approaches, and I know not how long I shall be detained here, I hope you will not impute this unceremonious treatment, to any want of respect in

Sir

Your most obedient and most humble Servant

Sam: Johnson[12]

[11] This accounts, perhaps, for the errors and the un-Johnsonian usages in this letter ("Dear Sir James," "have wrote," "illucidated," "Hool," "*Samuel* Johnson").

[12] Thrale won the election. He retained his seat, in fact, until 1780, the year before his death (see Letters 179, 189). Johnson often helped with his electioneering.

70. *To James Boswell*

Oxford, March 23, 1768

My dear Boswell,

I have omitted a long time to write to you, without knowing very well why. I could now tell why I should not write, for who would write to men who publish the letters of their friends without their leave? Yet I write to you in spite of my caution, to tell you that I shall be glad to see you, and that I wish you would empty your head of Corsica, which I think has filled it rather too long. But, at all events, I shall be glad, very glad, to see you.

I am, Sir,

Yours affectionately

Sam: Johnson[13]

71. *To Mrs. Thrale*

May 23, 1768

Madam

Though I purpose to come home tomorrow I would not omit even so long to tell you how much I think myself favoured by your notice. Every Man is desirous to keep those Friends whom he is proud to have gained, and I count the friendship of your house among the felicities of life.

I thank God that I am better, and am at least within hope of being as well as you have ever known me. Let me have your prayers.

I am Madam

Your most humble servant

Sam: Johnson

[13] See Letters 64 and 66.

72. *To Francis Barber, Bishop Stortford, Hertfordshire*[14]

May 28, 1768

Dear Francis

I have been very much out of order. I am glad to hear that you are well, and design to come soon to see you. I would have you stay at Mrs Clapp's for the present, till I can determine what we shall do. Be a good Boy.

My compliments to Mrs Clapp and to Mr Fowler.

I am Yours affectionately
Sam: Johnson

73. *To Mrs. Thrale*

Lichfield, August 14, 1769

Madam

I set out on Thursday Morning, and found my Companion, to whom I was very much a Stranger, more agreeable than I expected. We went cheerfully forward, and passed the night at Coventry. We came in late and went out early, and therefore I did not send for my Cousin Tom, but I design to make him some amends for the omission.

Next day we came early to Lucy who was, I believe, glad to see us. She had saved her best gooseberries upon the tree for me, and, as Steele says, *I was neither too proud nor too wise* to gather them. I have rambled a very little inter fontes et flumina nota,[15] but am not yet well. They have cut down the trees in George Lane. Evelyn in his book of forest trees tells us of wicked men that cut down trees and never prospered afterwards, yet nothing has deterred these audacious aldermen from violating the Hamadryads[16] of George Lane. As an impartial traveller I must however tell that in Stow street where I left a draw-well, I have found a pump, but the lading well in this ill-fated George Lane lyes shamefully neglected.

I am going to day or to morrow to Ashbourne, but I am at a loss how I shall get back in time to London. Here are only chance

[14] Johnson had sent his Negro servant Francis here to school.
[15] "Amid the fountains and the famous streams." (Virgil.)
[16] Wood nymphs; their lives, supposedly, are bound up with those of their trees.

Coaches, so that there is no certainty of a place. If I do not come, let it not hinder your journey. I can be but a few days behind you, and I will follow in the Brighthelmston Coach. But I hope to come.

I took care to tell Miss Porter, that I have got another Lucy.[17] I hope she is well. Tell Mrs. Salusbury that I beg her to stay at Streatham, for little Lucy's sake.

I am Madam
Your most obliged humble Servant
Sam: Johnson

74. *To Elizabeth Aston, Lichfield*

Brighthelmston, August 26, 1769

Madam

I suppose you have received the Mill. The whole apparatus seemed to be perfect, except that there is wanting a little tin spout at the bottom, and some ring or knob on which the bag, that catches the meal is to be hung.

When these are added, I hope you will be able to grind your own bread, and treat me with a cake made by yourself of meal, from your own corn of your own grinding.

I was glad, Madam, to see you so well, and hope your health will long encrease, and then long continue.

I am Madam
Your most obedient Servant
Sam: Johnson

75. *To James Boswell*

Brighthelmston, September 9, 1769

Dear Sir

Why do you charge me with unkindness? I have omitted nothing that could do you good, or give you pleasure, unless it be that I have forborne to tell you my opinion of your account of Corsica. I be-

---

[17] Lucy Elizabeth, the fifth of the Thrale's twelve children, was born on June 22.

lieve my opinion, if you think well of my judgement, might have given you pleasure; but when it is considered how much vanity is excited by praise, I am not sure that it would have done you good. Your History is like other histories, but your Journal is in a very high degree curious and delightful. There is between the history and the journal that difference which there will always be found between notions borrowed from without, and notions generated within. Your history was copied from books; your journal rose out of your own experience and observation. You express images which operated strongly upon yourself, and you have impressed them with great force upon your readers. I know not whether I could name any narrative by which curiosity is better excited, or better gratified.

I am glad that you are going to be married;[18] and as I wish you well in things of less importance, wish you well with proportionate ardour in this crisis of your life. What I can contribute to your happiness, I should be very unwilling to with-hold; for I have always loved and valued you, and shall love you and value you still more, as you become more regular and useful: effects which a happy marriage will hardly fail to produce.

I do not find that I am likely to come back very soon from this place. I shall, perhaps, stay a fortnight longer; and a fortnight is a long time to a lover absent from his mistress. Would a fortnight ever have an end?

I am, dear Sir,
Your most affectionate humble servant,
Sam. Johnson.

76. *To Edmund Burke*

June 21, 1770

Dear Sir,

I promised a long time ago to send you Cowley's Latin Works. If you have not yet seen them, be pleased to accept of this copy

[18] Boswell was married to Margaret Montgomerie on November 25.

which I bought in Oxford, and which is of the best edition. You may easily repay this little present by informing me that Dear Mrs. Burke is better. I am

Sir,

Your most humble servant

Sam: Johnson

77. *To Mrs. Thrale*

Ashbourne, July 23, 1770

Dearest Madam . . .

I have seen the great Bull, and very great he is.[19] I have seen likewise his heir apparent, who promises to inherit all the bulk and all the virtues of his Sire. I have seen the Man who offered an hundred guineas for the young Bull while he was yet little better than a Calf. Matlock I am afraid I shall not see, but I purpose to see Dovedale,[20] and after all this seeing I hope to see You.

I am Madam

Your most obliged humble Servant

Sam: Johnson

78. *To Bennet Langton, Langton*

March 20, 1771

Dear Sir

After much lingering of my own, and much of the Ministry, I have at length got out my paper. But delay is not yet at an end, not many had been dispersed before Lord North ordered the sale to stop. His reasons I do not distinctly know, you may try to find them in the perusal.[21] Before his order a sufficient number were dispersed

---

[19] Taylor's princely establishment at Ashbourne included "the largest horned cattle, I believe, in England, particularly a Bull of an enormous size." (Mrs. Thrale.)

[20] Scenic landmarks of Derbyshire.

[21] Lord North had withdrawn Johnson's political tract on the Falkland's Islands dispute because of an insulting reference to the late George Grenville.

to do all the mischief, though perhaps not to make all the sport that might be expected from it.

Soon after your departure I had the pleasure of finding all the danger past with which your navigation[22] was threatned. I hope nothing happens at home to abate your satisfaction, but that Lady Rothes, and Mrs Langton and the young Ladies are all well.

I was last night at the club. Dr. Percy has written a long Ballad in many *Fits;* it is pretty enough. He has printed, and will soon publish it. Goldsmith is at Bath with Lord Clare. At Mr. Thrale's, where I am now writing, all are well.

I am Dear Sir

Your most humble Servant

Sam: Johnson

79. *To the Comtesse de Boufflers*

May 16, 1771

Oui, Madame, le moment est arrivé, et il faut que je parte, mais pourquoi faut il partir? est ce que je m'ennuye? je m'ennuyerai ailleurs. est ce que je cherche ou quelque plaisir ou quelque soulagement? Je ne cherche rien, je n'espere rien. Aller, voir ce que j'ai vû, être un peu rejoué, un peu degouté, me resouvenir que la vie se passe et qu'elle se passe en vain, me plaindre de moi, m'endurcir aux dehors, voici le tout de ce qu'on compte pour les delices de l'année.

Que Dieu vous donne, Madame, tous les agremens de la vie, avec un esprit qui peut en jouir, sans s'y livrer trop.[23]

---

[22] I.e., canal.

[23] "Yes, Madame, the moment has arrived, and I must leave; but why must I leave? because I am bored? I would be bored anywhere. Because I am seeking some pleasure, some relief? I seek nothing, I hope for nothing. To go, to see what I have seen, to be cheered a bit, to be wearied a bit, to remind myself that life is passing and that it passes in vain, to lament my lot, to become hardened abroad, this is all one can expect for the year's delights.

"May God grant you, Madame, all the pleasures of life along with a spirit that can enjoy them, without giving in to them too much."

80. To Mrs. Thrale

Ashbourne, July 15, 1771

Dear Madam

When we come together to practice chymistry, I believe we shall find our furnaces sufficient for most operations.[24] We have a Gentleman here reading philosophical lectures, who performs the chymical part with furnaces of the same kind with ours, but much less, yet he says, that he can in his little furnace raise a fire that will melt iron. I saw him smelt lead, and shall bring up some oar for our operations. The carriage will cost more than the lead perhaps will be worth but a Chymist is very like a Lover

'And sees those dangers which he cannot shun.' [25]

I will try to get other oar both of iron and copper, which are all which this county affords, though feracissima metallorum regio.[26]

The Doctor has no park, but a little enclosure behind his house, in which there are about thirty Bucks and Does, and they take bread from the hand. Would it not be a pity to kill them? It seems to be now out of his head.

This day we had no strawberries.

I am Madam,

Your most obliged and most humble servant

Sam: Johnson

81. To Mrs. Thrale

Ashbourne, July 17, 1771

Madam

At Lichfield I found little to please me. One more of my few school fellows is dead, upon which I might make a new reflection,

[24] This is but one of the many evidences of Johnson's fascination for "chymical" experiments. Mr. Thrale had fitted out a full amateur's laboratory for him at Streatham.

[25] "And see the Folly, which I cannot shun." (Pope, "The Basset-Table.")

[26] "A district very rich in metals."

and say Mors omnibus communis.[27] Miss Porter was rather better than last year, but I think Miss Aston grows rather worse. I took a walk in quest of juvenile images, but caught a cloud instead of Juno.[28]

I longed for Taylor's chaise, but I think Lucy did not long for it, though she was not sorry to see it. Lucy is a Philosopher, and considers me as one of the external and accidental things that are to be taken and left without emotion. If I could learn of Lucy would it be better? Will you teach me? . . .

82. To Sir Joshua Reynolds

Ashbourne, July 17, 1771

Dear Sir

When I came to Lichfield I found that my portrait had been much visited and much admired. Every man has a lurking wish to appear considerable in his native place, and I was pleased with the dignity conferred by such a testimony of your regard.

Be pleased therefore to accept the thanks of

Sir

Your most obliged and most humble Servant,

Sam: Johnson.

Compliments to Miss Reynolds.

83. To David Garrick

Streatham, December 12, 1771

Dear Sir

I have thought upon your Epitaph, but without much effect. An Epitaph is no easy thing.

Of your three stanzas, the third is utterly unworthy of you. The first and third together give no discriminative character. If the first

[27] "Death is common to all."

[28] Jove thwarted an attempted rape on Juno by substituting a cloud in her likeness, deceiving her seducer.

alone were to stand, Hogarth would not be distinguished from any other man of intellectual eminence.

Suppose you worked upon something like this.

> The Hand of Art here torpid lies
> wav'd
> That traced th'essential form of Grace,[29]
> Here death has clos'd the curious eyes
> That saw the manners in the Face.

> If Genius warm thee, Reader, stay,
> If Merit touch thee, shed a tear,
> Be Vice and Dulness far away
> Great Hogarth's honour'd Dust is here.

In your second stanza *pictured Morals* is a beautifull expression, which I would wish to retain; but *learn* and *mourn* cannot stand for rhymes. *Art and Nature* have been seen together too often. In the first stanza is *feeling* in the second *feel*. *Feeling* for *tenderness* or *sensibility* is a word merely colloquial of late introduction, not yet sure enough of its own existence to claim a place upon a stone. *If thou hast neither,* is quite prose, and prose of the familiar kind.

Thus easy it is to find faults, but it is hard to make an epitaph.

When you have reviewed it, let me see it again, you are welcome to any help that I can give, on condition that you make my compliments to Mrs Garrick.

> I am Dear Sir
> Your most &c.,
> *Sam: Johnson*

---

[29] A reference to Hogarth's "Line of Beauty," an idealized S-curve he thought essential to a "beautiful" contour.

84. To Joseph Banks

February 27, 1772

'Perpetui, ambitâ bis terrâ, praemia lactis
    Haec habet, altrici Capra secunda Jovis.' [30]

Sir

I return thanks to you and to Dr. Solander for the pleasure which I received in yesterday's conversation. I could not recollect a motto for your Goat, but have given her a distich. You, Sir, may some time have an epick poem from some happier pen than that of

Sir,

Your most humble servant,

Sam: Johnson

85. To Robert Chambers, Oxford

April 11, 1772

Dear Sir . . .

I think nothing has happened here, but that Boswel is come up gratis with an appeal to the Lords. While I am writing I expect to hear him come in, with his noisy benevolence.

I am Sir

Your most humble servant

Sam: Johnson

86. To John Taylor, Westminster

April 17, 1772

Dear Sir

When I promised to dine with you to-morrow I did not sufficiently consider what I was promising. On the last day of Lent I do

[30] "After a double navigation of the globe, the goat, second only to she that nursed Jove, has this reward for her never-failing milk." This inscription was designed for the collar of Banks' goat, which had provided milk on shipboard on two round-the-world expeditions.

not willingly go out, and shall be glad to change to-morrow for Monday, or any other day except Thursday next week.

I am, Sir,

Your most, &c.

Sam: Johnson

87. *To John Taylor, Ashbourne*

August 31, 1772

Dear Sir . . .

Your uneasiness at the misfortunes of your Relations, I comprehend perhaps too well. It was an irresistible obtrusion of a disagreeable image, which you always wished away but could not dismiss, an incessant persecution of a troublesome thought neither to be pacified nor ejected. Such has of late been the state of my own mind. I had formerly great command of my attention, and what I did not like could forbear to think on. But of this power which is of the highest importance to the tranquillity of life, I have for some time past been so much exhausted, that I do not go into a company towards night in which I foresee anything disagreeable, nor enquire after any thing to which I am not indifferent, lest something, which I know to be nothing, should fasten upon my imagination, and hinder me from sleep. Thus it is that the progress of life brings often with it diseases not of the body only, but of the mind. We must endeavour to cure both the one and the other. In our bodies we must ourselves do a great part, and for the mind it is very seldom that any help can be had, but what prayer and reason shall supply.

I have got my work so far forward that I flatter myself with concluding it this month, and then shall do nothing so willingly as come down to Ashbourne. We will try to make October a pleasant month.

I am, Sir,

Yours affectionately

Sam: Johnson

88. To Hester Maria ("Queeney") Thrale[31]

Ashbourne, November 2, 1772

Dear Sweeting

Your pretty letter was too short. If Lucy is not good, you must try to mend her by good advice, and good example, for all the little girls will try to be like you. I am glad to hear of the improvement and prosperity of my hen. Miss Porter has buried her fine black cat. So things come and go. Generations, as Homer says, are but like leaves; and you now see the faded leaves falling about you.

You are sorry to come to town, and I am sorry for dear Granmamma that will be left in the country, be sure that you make my compliments to her.

> I am, Dear Miss,
> Your most obedient servant
> *Sam: Johnson*

89. To Mrs. Thrale

Ashbourne, November 27, 1772

Dear Madam . . .

I was yesterday at Chatsworth.[32] It is a very fine house. I wish you had been with me to see it, for then, as we are apt to want matter of talk, we should have gained something new to talk on. They complimented me with playing the fountains, and opening the cascade. But I am of my friend's opinion, that when one has seen the Ocean, cascades are but little things. . . .

90. To Hester Maria Thrale

Ashbourne, November 28, 1772

Dear Miss,

Mamma used us both very sorrily when she hindered you from writing to me. She does not know how much I should love to read your letters, if they were a little longer. But we shall soon, I hope,

---

[31] She was then eight years old.

[32] The palatial seventeenth-century seat of the Dukes of Devonshire.

talk matters all over. I have not had the luck this journey to pick up any curiosities for the cabinet. I would have been glad to bring you something, if I could have found it.

I hope you go often to see dear Grandmamma. We must all do what we can to help her and please her, and take great care now she is so bad, not to make her worse.

You said nothing of Lucy, I suppose she is grown a pretty good scholar, and a very good playfellow; after dinner we shall have good sport playing all together, and we will none of us cry.

Make my compliments to Grandmamma, and Papa, and Mamma, and all the young ones.

I am Dearest Miss,
Your most humble servant,
Sam: Johnson

91. To Mrs. Thrale

January 26, 1773

Madam

The inequalities of human life have always employed the meditation of deep thinkers, and I cannot forbear to reflect on the differ-ence between your condition and my own. You live upon mock turtle, and stewed rumps of beef; I dined yesterday upon crumpets. You sit with parish officers, caressing and caressed, the idol of the table, and the wonder of the day. I pine in the solitude of sickness, not bad enough to be pitied, and not well enough to be endured. You sleep away the night, and laugh or scold away the day. I cough and grumble, and grumble and cough. Last night was very tedious, and this day makes no promises of much ease. However I have this day put on my shoe, and hope that Gout is gone. I shall have only the cough to contend with, and I doubt whether I shall get rid of that without change of place. I caught cold in the coach as I went away, and am disordered by very little things. Is it accident or age?

I am, dearest Madam,
Your most obedient and most humble servant
Sam: Johnson

1763-1773

92. To James Boswell, Edinburgh

February 24, 1773

Dear Sir . . .

I have heard of your masquerade. What says your Synod [33] to such innovations? I am not studiously scrupulous, nor do I think a masquerade either evil in itself, or very likely to be the occasion of evil; yet as the world thinks it a very licentious relaxation of manners, I would not have been one of the *first* masquers in a country where no masquerade had ever been before.

A new edition of my great[34] Dictionary is printed, from a copy which I was persuaded to revise; but having made no preparation, I was able to do very little. Some superfluities I have expunged, and some faults I have corrected, and here and there have scattered a remark; but the main fabrick of the work remains as it was. I had looked very little into it since I wrote it, and, I think, I found it full as often better, as worse, than I expected.

Baretti and Davies have had a furious quarrel; a quarrel, I think, irreconcileable. Dr. Goldsmith has a new comedy, which is expected in the spring. No name is yet given it.[35] The chief diversion arises from a stratagem by which a lover is made to mistake his future father-in-law's house for an inn. This, you see, borders upon farce. The dialogue is quick and gay, and the incidents are so prepared as not to seem improbable. . . .

93. To the Reverend William White, Philadelphia

March 4, 1773

Dear Sir

Your kindness for your friends accompanies you cross the Atlantick. It was long since observed by Horace, that no ship could leave care behind, you have been attended in your voyage by better pow-

[33] I.e., the Scotch Presbyterian Church.
[34] I.e., the large folio version.
[35] *She Stoops to Conquer.* The name was not decided on until the very last minute.

ers, by Benevolence and Constancy, and I hope Care did not often show her face in their company.

I received the copy of Rasselas. The impression is not magnificent, but it flatters an Authour, because the Printer seems to have expected that it would be scattered among the People. The little Book has been well received, and is translated into Italian, French, German, and Dutch. It has now one honour more by an American Edition.

I know not that much has happened since your departure, that can engage your curiosity. Of all publick transactions the whole world is now informed by the Newspapers. Opposition seems to despond, and the Dissenters though they have taken advantage of unsettled times, and a government much enfeebled, seem not likely to gain any immunities.

Dr. Goldsmith has a new comedy in rehearsal at Covent garden, to which the Manager predicts ill success. I hope he will be mistaken. I think it deserves a very kind reception.

I shall soon publish a new Edition of my large Dictionary; I have been persuaded to revise it, and have mended some faults, but added little to its usefulness.

No book has been published since your departure of which much notice is taken. Faction only fills the town with Pamphlets, and greater subjects are forgotten in the noise of discord.

Thus have I written only to tell you how little I have to tell. Of myself I can only add that having been afflicted many weeks with a very troublesome cough, I am now recovered.

I take the liberty which you give me of troubling you with a letter, of which you will please to fill up the direction.

I am Sir
Your most humble Servant,
Sam: Johnson

94. *To Oliver Goldsmith*

April 23, 1773

Sir

I beg that you will excuse my Absence to the Club. I am going this evening to Oxford.

I have another favour to beg. It is that I may be considered as proposing Mr. Boswel for a candidate of our Society, and that he may be considered as regularly nominated.

I am, Sir,
Your most humble Servant
Sam: Johnson

95. *To Mrs. Thrale*

(May 1773?)

Madame trés honorée[36]

Puisque, pendant que je me trouve chez vous, il faut passer, tous les jours, plusieures heures dans une solitude profonde, dites moi, Si vous voulez que je vogue a plein abandon, ou que je me contienne dans des bornes prescrites. S'il vous plaît, ma tres chere maîtresse, que je sois lassè a hazard. La chose est faite. Vous vous souvenez de la sagesse de nôtre ami, *Si je ferai &c.* Mais, si ce n'est trop d'esperer que je puisse être digne, comme auparavant, des soins et de la protection d'une ame si aimable par sa douceur, et si venerable par son elevation, accordez moi, par un petit ecrit, la connoissance de ce que m'est permis, et que m'est interdit. Et s'il vous semble mieux que je demeure dans un certain lieu, je vous supplie de m'epargner la neces-

---

[36] "Most honored Madam

Since, while I find myself among you, I am obliged to pass several hours every day in a deep solitude, tell me, if you want me to course freely, where I may confine myself within prescribed bounds. If you wish, my dearest mistress, that I be left to chance, it will be done. You recall the wisdom of our friend, *'If I should make etc.'* But, if it is not too much to hope that I may be worthy, as heretofore, of the care and protection of a soul so amiable for its sweetness, and so venerable for its elevation, grant me, by a little note, to know what is permitted me, and what is forbidden. And if it seems preferable to you for me to stay in a particular place, I beg you to spare me the obligation of constraining myself, by taking away from me the power

sitè de me contraindre, en m'ôtant le pouvoir de sortir d'ou vou voulez que je sois. Ce que vous ne coûtera que la peine de tourner le clef dans la porte, deux fois par jour. Il faut agir tout a fait en Maîtresse, afin que vôtre jugement et vôtre vigilance viennent a secours de ma faiblesse.

Pour ce que regarde la table, j'espere tout de vôtre sagesse et je crains tout de vôtre douceur. Tournez, Madame tres honorèe, vos pensèes de ce côte la. Il n'y a pour vous rien de difficile; vous pourrez inventer une regime pratiquable sans bruît, et efficace sans peril.

Est ce trop de demander d'une ame telle qu'est la vôtre, que, maîtresse des autres, elle devienne maîtresse de soy-même, et qu'elle triomphe de cette inconstance, qui a fait si souvent, qu'elle a negligèe l'execution de ses propres loix, qu'elle a oublièe tant de promesses, et qu'elle m'a condamnè a tant de solicitations reiterèes que la resouvenance me fait horreur. Il faut ou accorder, ou refuser; il faut

---

of leaving the place where you want me to be. This will cost you no more than the effort of turning the key in the door, two times a day. You must act the Mistress completely, so that your judgment and your vigilance may come to the aid of my weakness.

As for meals, I hope for everything from your wisdom, and I fear everything from your kindness. Turn your thoughts in this direction, most honored Madam. There is no difficulty here for you; you will be able to devise a diet that is practical without ado, efficacious without danger.

Is it too much to beg of a soul such as yours, that, mistress of others, she become mistress of herself, and that she triumph over that inconstancy which has allowed her so often to neglect the execution of her own laws, to forget so many promises, and to condemn me to solicitations repeated so many times that the recollection of them fills me with horror? You must either grant me this, or refuse me; and you must remember what you grant. I want always to be sensible of your rule, my patroness, and I want you to hold me in that slavery which you know so well how to render pleasant.

Allow me the honor to be, Madam, your most obedient servant."

This note is, obviously, confusing; perhaps due to Johnson's weak French, perhaps (Chapman) "studiously enigmatic." The confusion, as well as the French, may be explained by Johnson's difficulty in expressing himself on so sensitive an issue.

The vague hints of "imprisonment" in this letter are confirmed, how-se souvenir de ce qu'on accorde. Je souhaite, ma patronne, que vôtre autoritè me soit toûjours sensible, et que vous me tieniez dans l'esclavage que vou scavez si bien rendre heureuse.

Permettez moi l'honeur d'être Madame

Vôtre très obeissant serviteur

---

ever, by Johnson's diary notations ("De pedicis et manicis insana cogitatio": "Mad thoughts of fetters and handcuffs," May 24, 1771); by the record of a sale of "Johnson's Padlock"; by his letter of May 29 ("I long to be in my own room. Have you got your key?"); and especially by Mrs. Thrale's "petit ecrit" of answer:

. . . [You] brood in secret upon an Idea hateful in itself, but which your kind partiality to me has unhappily rendered pleasing. If it be possible shake off these uneasy Weights, heavier to the Mind by far than Fetters to the body. Let not your fancy dwell thus upon Confinement and Severity. I am sorry you are obliged to be so much alone; I foresaw some ill Consequences of your being here while my Mother was dying thus; yet could not resist the temptation of having you near me, but if you find this irksome and dangerous Idea fasten upon your fancy, leave me to struggle with the loss of one Friend, and let me not put to hazard what I esteem beyond Kingdoms, and value beyond the possession of them.

If we go on together your Confinement shall be as strict as possible except when Company comes in, which I shall more willingly endure on your Account.

Dissipation is to you a glorious Medicine, and I believe Mr Boswell will be at last your best Physician. for the rest you really are well enough now if you will keep so; and not suffer the noblest of human Minds to be tortured with fantastic notions which rob it of all its Quiet. I will detain you no longer, so farewell and be good; and do not quarrell with your Governess for not using the Rod enough
—H:L:T.

Johnson, apparently, for fear of insanity, had himself kept at times a locked prisoner at Streatham.

July 1773-January 1774

Four different works—two rough drafts and two finished books—grew out of Johnson's extraordinary three-month tour through Scotland with Boswell in the fall of 1773. There is Boswell's extensive journal of the trip, unpublished until 1936. "Boswell writes a regular journal of our travels, which, I think, contains as much of what I say and do, as of all other occurrences together." The polished and chastened reduction of this manuscript, called The Journal of a Tour to the Hebrides with Samuel Johnson, LL.D., *was published by Boswell in 1786, giving Englishmen a foretaste of what the great* Life *was to be like. Johnson's own version of the tour was published in 1774; he called it* A Journey to the Western Islands of Scotland. *And his letters (100 to 108) to the Thrales from*

95

Scotland, together with a lost "book of remarks," served as a first draft for the Journey.

This Scottish tour had first been suggested (by Johnson) some ten years before, within three months of his first meeting Boswell. That Boswell encouraged the notion is not surprising; what is surprising is that Johnson, now sixty-four years old, diseased and melancholic, so in love with his London and his creature comforts, should have agreed to go—in fact seized at the chance; and, finally, should have loved it, despite the rotten weather and barren prospects, the straw beds, the deceitful Presbyterian Scots. "He often said to me, that the time he spent in this Tour was the pleasantest part of his life, and asked me if I would lose the recollection of it for five hundred pounds."

It may simply have been that for once his mind was safely filled, his imagination directed outward. Variety and good company were assured for a hundred days. While his huge body bounced over bumpy wet islands on wobbling little horses, his mind could be at ease. He could verify his prejudices (always a delightful enterprise) about Scotsmen and Scotland, inspect a dying primitive order with a biased anthropologist's eye, and witness the Grand Principle of Subordination in its purest, most archaic European form among the chieftains and clans of the Western Isles.

Like Imlac's Poet, he tried to learn everything. He saw the sights, he measured ruins, he investigated legends and rumors, he questioned his hosts endlessly on a hundred topics—history, geography, politics, religion, manners, language, entertainments, agriculture, commerce, the social classes, eating habits, the popular superstitions. It is all there in the Journey, *turned into stately Johnsonese, and intoned with a sad nostalgia for the feudal way of life. It is all here, too, in the long letters to Mrs. Thrale, letters less finished and sententious, on the whole, than the* Journey, *and slightly more alive.*

For once, on this odd excursion, Johnson was able to see himself from the outside, as Boswell saw him, as we see him, and laugh at the spectacle of Samuel Johnson rambling his ungainly way about a circuit now marked by "Johnson Slept Here" plaques on innkeepers' walls. "I cannot think many things here more likely to affect the fancy, than to see Johnson ending his sixty fourth year in the wilderness of the Hebrides," he wrote. *"I cannot but laugh, to think of myself roving among the Hebrides at sixty. I wonder where I shall rove at fourscore?"*

96. To James Boswell, Edinburgh

July 5, 1773

Dear Sir

When your letter came to me, I was so darkened by an inflammation in my eye, that I could not for some time read it. I can now write without trouble, and can read large prints. My eye is gradually growing stronger; and I hope will be able to take some delight in the survey of a Caledonian loch.

Chambers is going a Judge, with six thousand a year, to Bengal. He and I shall come down together as far as Newcastle, and thence I shall easily get to Edinburgh. Let me know the exact time when your Courts intermit. I must conform a little to Chambers's occasions, and he must conform a little to mine. The time which you shall fix, must be the common point to which we will come as near as we can. Except this eye, I am very well. . . .

97. To James Boswell, Edinburgh

August 3, 1773

Dear Sir

I shall set out from London on Friday the sixth of this month, and purpose not to loiter much by the way. Which day I shall be at Edinburgh, I cannot exactly tell. I suppose I must drive to an inn, and send a porter to find you.

I am afraid Beattie will not be at his College soon enough for us, and I shall be sorry to miss him; but there is no staying for the concurrence of all conveniences. We will do as well as we can.

I am, Sir,

Your most humble servant,

Sam. Johnson.

98. To James Boswell, Edinburgh

Newcastle, August 11, 1773

Dear Sir

I came hither last night, and hope, but do not absolutely promise, to be in Edinburgh on Saturday. Beattie will not come so soon.

I am, Sir,
Your most humble servant,
Sam. Johnson

My compliments to your lady.

99. To James Boswell

Edinburgh, August 14, 1773

Mr. Johnson sends his compliments to Mr. Boswell, being just arrived at Boyd's.

Saturday night.

100. To Mrs. Thrale

Bamff, August 25, 1773

Dear Madam . . .

August 18. I passed with Boswel the Firth of Forth, and began our Journey. In the passage We observed an Island which I persuaded my companions to survey. We found it to be a Rock somewhat troublesome to climb, about a mile long and half a mile broad; in the middle were the ruins of an old fort, which had on one of the stones Maria Re. 1564. It had been only a blockhouse one story high. I measured two apartments of which the walls were entire and found them 27 feet long and 23 broad. The Rock had some grass and many thistles, both cows and sheep were grazing. There was a spring of water. The name is Inchkeith. Look on your Maps.

. . . we came late to St. Andrews, the most ancient of the Scotch universities, and once the See of the Primate of Scotland. The inn was full, but Lodgings were provided for us at the house of the professor of Rhetorick, a Man of elegant manners who showed us in the morning the poor remains of a stately Cathedral, demolished in

Knox's reformation, and now only to be imaged by tracing its foundation and contemplating the little ruins that are left.[1] Here was once a religious house. Two of the vaults or cellars of the Subprior are yet entire. In one of them lives an old Woman who claims an hereditary residence in it, boasting that her husband was the sixth tenant of this gloomy mansion in a lineal descent, and claiming by her marriage with this Lord of the cavern, an alliance with the Bruces. Mr. Boswel staid a while to interrogate her, because he understood her language. She told him, that she and her Cat lived together; that she had two sons somewhere, who might perhaps be dead; that when there were quality in the town, notice was taken of her; and that now she was neglected, but did not trouble them. . . .

[August] 21 We travelled towards Aberdeen, another University, and in the way dined at Lord Monbodo's, the Scotch Judge who has lately written a strange book about the origin of Language, in which he traces Monkeys up to Men, and says that in some countries the human species have tails like other beasts. He enquired for these longtailed Men of Banks, and was not well pleased, that they had not been found in all his peregrination. He talked nothing of this to me, and I hope, we parted friends, for we agreed pretty well, only we differed in adjusting the claims of merit between a Shopkeeper of London, and a Savage of the American wildernesses. Our opinions were, I think, maintained on both sides without full conviction; Monbodo declared boldly for the Savage, and I perhaps for that reason sided with the Citizen. . . .[2]

[1] At this point in his *Journey* Johnson injected a bitter paragraph on the "epidemical enthusiasm, compounded of sullen scrupulousness and warlike ferocity" of the Scottish reformers.

[2] This was an instance of Boswell's arrangement of encounters between Johnson and his enemies, of which the dinner with Wilkes was the most famous. "I knew Lord Monboddo and Dr. Johnson did not love each other; yet I was unwilling not to visit his Lordship; and was also curious to see them together." (Boswell's *Tour*.)

101. To Mrs. Thrale

Inverness, August 28, 1773

Dearest Madam

August. 23. I had the honour of attending the Lord Provost of Aberdeen, and was presented with the freedom of the city, not in a gold box but in good Latin. Let me pay Scotland one just praise. There was no officer gaping for a fee; this could have been said of no city on the English side of the Tweed. I wore my patent of freedom *pro more*[3] in my hat from the New town to the Old about a mile. I then dined with my friend the Professor of Physick at his house, and saw the King's College.

Boswell was very angry that the Aberdeen professors would not talk. . . .

102. To Mrs. Thrale

Armadale in Skye, September 6, 1773

Dearest Madam

I am now looking on the Sea from a house of Sir Alexander Macdonald in the Isle of Skie. Little did I once think of seeing this region of obscurity, and little did you once expect a salutation from this verge of European Life. I have now the pleasure of going where nobody goes, and of seeing what nobody sees. Our design is to visit several of the smaller Islands, and then pass over to the South west of Scotland. . . .

August 26 We dined at Elgin where we saw the ruins of a noble Cathedral. The Chapterhouse is yet standing. A great part of Elgin is built with small piazzas to the lower story. We went on to Foris over the heath where Macbeth met the witches, but had no adven-

[3] According to custom. "It was striking to hear all of them drinking 'Dr. Johnson! Dr. Johnson!' in the town-hall of Aberdeen, and then to see him with his burgess-ticket, or diploma, in his hat, which he wore as he walked along the street, according to the usual custom." (Boswell's *Tour*.)

ture.[4] Only in the way we saw for the first time some houses with fruit trees about them. The improvements of the Scotch are for immediate profit they do not yet think it worth while to plant what will not produce something to be eaten or sold in a very little time. We rested at Foris.

A very great proportion of the people are barefoot, and if one may judge by the rest of the dress, to send out boys without shoes into the streets or ways. There are however more beggars than I have ever seen in England; they beg, if not silently, yet very modestly. . . .

[August 28] At night we came to Inverness, the last considerable town in the North, where we staid all the next day, for it was Sunday, and saw the ruins of what is called Macbeth's Castle. It never was a large house, but was strongly situated. From Inverness we were to travel on Horseback.

Aug. 30. We set out with four horses. We had two Highlanders to run by us, who were active, officious, civil, and hardy. Our Journey was for many miles along a military way made upon the bank of Lough Ness,[5] a Water about eighteen miles long, but not, I think, half a mile broad. Our horses were not bad, and the way was very pleasant. The rock out of which the road was cut was covered with Birch trees, fern and heath. The Lake below was beating its bank by a gentle wind, and the rocks beyond the water on the right, stood sometimes horrid and wild and sometimes opened into a kind of bay in which there was a spot of cultivated ground, yellow with corn. In one part of the way we had trees on both sides, for perhaps half a mile. Such a length of Shade perhaps Scotland cannot show in any other place.

You are not to suppose that here are to be any more towns or Inns. We came to a cottage which they call the Generals hut; where we alighted to dine, and had Eggs and Bacon, and Mutton, with wine, rum, and whiskey. I had water.

[4] "How far is't called to Fores? What are these,
   So wither'd, and so wild in their attire?
   That look not like the inhabitants o'the earth,
   And yet are on't."   [*Macbeth*, I, iii]
   [5] Loch Ness, lately home of the monster. He expands it, in the *Journey*, to 24 miles long, one to two miles broad.

At a bridge over the river which runs into the Ness, the rocks rise on three sides with a direction almost perpendicular to a great height, they are in part covered with trees, and exhibit a kind of dreadful magnificence. Standing like the barriers of nature placed to keep different orders of Being in perpetual separation. Near this Bridge is the fall of Fiers, a famous Cataract, of which by clambering over the rocks we obtained the view. The water was low, and therefore we had only the pleasure of knowing that rain would make it at once pleasing and formidable. There will then be a mighty flood foaming along a rocky channel frequently obstructed by protuberances, and exasperated by reverberation, at last precipitated with a sudden descent, and lost in the depth of a gloomy chasm.

We came somewhat late to Fort Augustus where the Lieutenant Governor met us beyond the gates, and apologised that at that hour he could not by the rule of a Garrison admit us otherwise than at a narrow door which only one can enter at a time. We were well entertained and well lodged, and next morning after having viewed the fort we persued our journey.

Our way now lay over the mountains, which were to be passed not by climbing them directly, but by traversing, so that as we went forward, we saw our baggage following us below in a direction exactly contrary. There is in these ways much labour but little danger, and perhaps other places of which very terrifick representations are made, are not in themselves more formidable. These roads have all been made by hewing the rock away with pickaxes, or bursting them with Gunpowder. The stones so separated are often piled loose as a wall by the way side. We saw an inscription importing the year in which one of the regiments made two thousand yards of the road Eastward.

After tedious travel of some hours we came to what, I believe, we must call a village, a place where there were three huts built of turf, at one of which we were to have our dinner and our bed, for we could not reach any better place that night. This place is called Enock in Glenmorrison. The house in which we lodged was distinguished by a chimney, the rest had only a hole for the smoke. Here we had Eggs, and Mutton, and a chicken, and a sausage, and rum. In the afternoon tea was made by a very decent Girl in a printed Linen. She engaged me so much that I made her a present of Cocker's Arithmetick.

> I am, Madam,
> Your most &c
> *Sam: Johnson*

103. To Mrs. Thrale

Dunvegan in Skye, September 15-21, 1773

Dearest Madam

I am so vexed at the necessity of sending yesterday so short a Letter that I purpose to get a long letter beforehand by writing something every day, which I may the more easily do, as a cold makes me now too deaf to take the usual pleasure in conversation. Lady Macleod is very kind to me, and the place at which we now are, is equal in strength of situation, in the wildness of the adjacent country, and in the plenty and elegance of the domestick entertainment, to a Castle in Gothick romances. The sea with a little Island is before us, cascades play within view. Close to the house is the formidable skeleton of an old Castle probably Danish; and the whole mass of building stands upon a protuberance of rock, inaccessible till of late but by a pair of stairs on the sea side, and secure in ancient times against any Enemy that was likely to invade the kingdom of Skie. Macleod has offered me an Island,[6] if it were not too far off I should hardly refuse it; my Island would be pleasanter than Brighthelmston, if you and Master could come to it, but I cannot think it pleasant to live quite alone. Oblitusque meorum, obliviscendus et illis.[7] That I should be elated by the dominion of an Island to

[6] "There is a beautiful little island in the Loch of Dunvegan, called *Isa*. M'Leod said, he would give it to Dr. Johnson, on the condition of his residing on it three months in the year; nay one month. Dr. Johnson was highly amused with the fancy . . . He talked a great deal of this island; —how he would have cannon,—how he would plant,—how he would sally out, and *take* the isle of Muck;—and then he laughed with uncommon glee, and could hardly leave off." (Boswell's *Tour*.)

[7] "My own forgetting, by my own forgot." (Horace.)

forgetfulness of my friends at Streatham, and I hope never to deserve that they should be willing to forget me. . . .

[September 1] About noon, we came to a small glen, so they call a valley, which compared with other places appeared rich and fertile. Here our Guides desired us to stop that the horses might graze, for the journey was very laborious, and no more grass would be found. We made no difficulty of compliance, and I sat down to take notes on a green bank, with a small stream running at my feet, in the midst of savage solitude, with Mountains before me, and on either hand covered with heath. I looked round me, and wondered that I was not more affected . . .

I cannot forbear to interrupt my Narrative. Boswel, with some of his troublesome kindness, has informed this family, and reminded me that the eighteenth of September is my birthday. The return of my Birthday, if I remember it, fills me with thoughts which it seems to be the general care of humanity to escape. I can now look back upon threescore and four years, in which little has been done, and little has been enjoyed, a life diversified by misery, spent part in the sluggishness of penury, and part under the violence of pain, in gloomy discontent, or importunate distress. But perhaps I am better than I should have been, if I had been less afflicted. With this I will try to be content. . . .

Towards Night we came to a very formidable Hill called Rattiken, which we climbed with more difficulty than we had yet experienced,[8] and at last came to Glanelg a place on the Seaside opposite to Skie. We were by this time weary and disgusted, nor was our humour much mended, by an inn, which, though it was built with lime and slate, the highlander's description of a house which he thinks magnificent, had neither wine, bread, eggs, nor any thing that we could eat or drink. When we were taken up stairs, a dirty fellow bounced out of the bed in which one of us was to lie. Boswel blustered, but nothing could be got. At last a Gentleman in the Neighbourhood who heard of our arrival sent us rum and white sugar. Boswel was now provided for in part, and the Landlord prepared some mutton chops, which we could not eat, and killed two Hens,

[8] "As Dr. Johnson is a great weight, the two guides agreed that he should ride the horses alternately." (Boswell's *Tour.*)

of which Boswel made his servant broil a limb, with what effect I know not. We had a lemon, and a piece of bread, which supplied me with my supper.

When the repast was ended, we began to deliberate upon bed. Mrs Boswel had warned us that we should *catch something*, and had given us Sheets for our security; for Sir Alexander and Lady Macdonald, she said, came back from Skie, so scratching themselves—. I thought sheets a slender defence, against the confederacy with which we were threatned, and by this time our highlanders had found a place where they could get some hay; I ordered hay to be laid thick upon the bed, and slept upon it in my great coat. Boswell laid sheets upon his hay, and reposed in Linen like a Gentleman. The horses were turned out to grass, with a man to watch them. The hill Ratiken, and the inn at Glanelg, are the only things of which we or travellers yet more delicate, could find any pretensions to complain.

Sept. 2. I rose rustling from the hay, and went to tea, which I forget whether we found or brought. We saw the Isle of Skie before us darkening the horizon with its rocky coast. A boat was procured, and we launched into one of the Straits of the Atlantick Ocean. We had a passage of about twelve miles to the point where Sir Alexander resided, having come from his Seat in the midland part, to a small house on the shore, as we believe, that he might with less reproach entertain us meanly. If he aspired to meanness his retrograde ambition was completely gratified, but he did not succeed equally in escaping reproach. He had no cook, nor, I suppose, much provision, nor had the Lady the common decencies of her tea table. We picked up our Sugar with our fingers. Boswel was very angry, and reproached him with his improper parsimony.[9] I did not much reflect upon the conduct of a man with whom I was not likely to converse as long at any other time. . . .

On Sept. 6. We left Macdonald, to visit Raarsa,[10] the Island which

[9] Boswell's remarks in his *Tour* on MacDonald's parsimony and lack of concern for his tenants nearly resulted in a duel. Johnson omits the derogatory reference from the *Journey*, but his private comments, recorded in Boswell's Manuscript Journal, were insulting enough.

[10] Raasay.

I have already mentioned. We were to cross part of Skie on horseback, a mode of travelling very uncomfortable, for the road is so narrow, where any road can be found that only one can go, and so craggy that the attention can never be remitted, it allows therefore neither the gayety of conversation nor the laxity of solitude, nor has it in itself the amusement of much variety, as it affords only all the possible transpositions of Bog, Rock, and Rivulet. Twelve Miles, by computation, make a reasonable journey for a day.

At night we came to a tenants house of the first rank of tenants where we were entertained better than the Landlords. There were books, both English and Latin. Company gathered about us, and we heard some talk of the Second sight[11] and some talk of the events of forty five,[12] a year which will not soon be forgotten among the Islanders. The next day we were confined by a storm, the company, I think, encreased and our entertainment was not only hospitable but elegant. At night, a Minister's sister in very fine Brocade, sung Earse[13] songs. I wished to know the meaning, but the Highlanders are not much used to scholastick questions, and no translation could be obtained.

Next day, Sept. 8. The weather allowed us to depart, a good boat was provided us, and we went to Raarsa, under the conduct of Mr Malcolm Macleod, a Gentleman who conducted Prince Charles through the mountains in his distresses. The prince, he says, was more active than himself, they were at least one night, without any shelter. . . .

I am Madam
Your most obedient servant
Sam: Johnson

We are this morning trying to get out of Skie.

[11] "The *Second Sight* is an impression made either by the mind upon the eye, or by the eye upon the mind, by which things distant or future are perceived, and seen as if they were present." (*Journey.*) Johnson had a lingering urge to believe in such apparitions all his life, and continually sought out evidence. "I never could advance my curiosity to conviction; but came away at last only willing to believe."
[12] The attempted invasion of the Stuart Pretender, Prince Charles, in 1745. Many Scotsmen had rallied to his cause.
[13] Scottish Gaelic.

104. To Mrs. Thrale

Talisker in Skye, September 24, 1773

Dear Madam

I am still in Skie. Do you remember the Song?

> Ev'ry Island is a prison
> Strongly guarded by the sea.

. . . We were received at Raarsa, on the sea-side, and after clambering with some difficulty over the rocks, a labour which the traveller wherever he reposes himself on land, must in these islands, be contented to endure, we were introduced into the house, which one of the company called the court of Raarsa, with politeness, which not the court of Versailles could have thought defective. The house is not large though we were told in our passage that it had eleven fire rooms, nor magnificently furnished, but our utensils were commonly silver. We went up into a dining room about as large as your blue room, where we had something given us to eat, and tea and coffee.[14]

Raarsa himself is a man of no inelegant appearance, and of manners uncomonly refined. Lady Raarsa makes no very sublime appearance for a Sovereign, but is a good Housewife, and a very prudent and diligent conductress of her family. Miss Flora Macleod is a celebrated Beauty, has been admired at Edinburgh, dresses her head very high, and has manners so Ladylike, that I wish her head-dress was lower. . . .

105. To Mrs. Thrale

Ostig in Skye, September 30, 1773

Dearest Madam

I am still confined in Skie. We were unskilful travellers, and imagined that the sea was an open road, which we could pass at pleasure, but we have now learned with some pain, that we may still wait

[14] Boswell noted, however, "the lack of a certain accommodation rarely to be found at the modern houses of Scotland, and which Dr. Johnson and I sought for in vain at the Laird of Rasáy's new-built mansion." (Boswell's *Tour*.)

for a long time the caprices of the equinoctial winds, and sit reading or writing as I now do, while the tempest is rolling the sea, and roaring in the mountains. I am now no longer pleased with the delay . . .

[September 12] We dined at a publick house at Portre; so called because one of the Scottish Kings landed there, in a progress through the Western Isles. Raarsa paid the reckoning privately. We then got on horseback, and by a short, but very tedious journey, came to Kingsburgh, at which the same King lodged after he landed. Here I had the honour of saluting the far famed Miss Flora Macdonald, who conducted the Prince dressed as her Maid through the English forces from the Island of Lewes, and when she came to Skie, dined with the English officers, and left her Maid below. She must then have been a young Lady, she is now not old, of a pleasing person and elegant behaviour. She told me that she thought herself honoured by my visit, and I am sure that whatever regard she bestowed on me, was liberally repaid. 'If thou likest her opinions thou wilt praise her virtue.' She was carried to London, but dismissed without a trial, and came down with Malcolm Macleod, against whom sufficient evidence could not be procured. She and her husband are poor, and are going to try their fortune in America. Sic rerum volvitur orbis.[15]

At Kingsburgh we were very liberally feasted, and I slept in the bed, on which the Prince reposed in his distress. The sheets which he used were never put to any meaner offices, but were wrapped up by the Lady of the house, and at last, according to her desire, were laid round her in her grave. These are not Whigs.[16]

On the 13th, travelling partly on horseback where we could not row, and partly on foot where we could not ride, we came to Dunvegan, which I have described already. Here though poor Macleod has been left by his Grandfather overwhelmed with debts, we had

[15] "So rolls the world."
[16] "To see Dr. Samuel Johnson lying in that bed, in the Isle of Sky, in the house of Miss Flora Macdonald, struck me with such a group of ideas as it is not easy for words to describe, as they passed through the mind. He smiled, and said, 'I have had no ambitious thoughts in it.'" (Boswell's *Tour*.)

another exhibition of feudal hospitality. There were two Stags in the house, and venison came to the table every day in its various forms. Macleod, besides his Estate in Skie, larger, I suppose than some English Counties, is Proprietor of nine inhabited Islands; and of his Islands uninhabited I doubt if he very exactly knows the number. I told him that he was a mighty monarch. Such dominions fill an Englishman with envious wonder, but when he surveys the naked mountain and treads the quaking moor, and wanders over wide regions of gloomy barrenness his wonder may continue, but his envy ceases. . . .

Sept. 23. We removed to Talisker a house occupied by Mr Macleod, a Lieutenant colonel in the Dutch service. Talisker has been long in the hands of Gentlemen, and therefore has a garden well cultivated, and what is here very rare, is shaded by trees. A place where the imagination is more amused cannot easily be found. The Mountains about it are of great height, with waterfals succeeding one another so fast, that as one ceases to be heard another begins; between the mountains there is a small valley extended to the sea, which is not far off beating upon a coast very difficult of access. Two nights before our arrival two boats were driven upon this coast by the tempest, one of them had a pilot that knew the passage, the second followed, but a third missed the true course, and was driven forward with great danger of being forced into the great Ocean, but however gained at last some other Island. The crews crept to Talisker almost lifeless with wet, cold, fatigue, and terrour, but the Lady took care of them. She is a woman of more than common qualifications; having travelled with her husband, she speaks four languages. . . .

We have now with us the young Laird of *Col*, who is heir perhaps to two hundred square miles of land. He has first studied at Aberdeen, and afterwards gone to Hertfordshire to learn agriculture, being much impressed with desire of improvement. He likewise has the notions of a Chief, and keeps a piper. At Macleods the bagpipe always plaid while we were dining.

Col has undertaken, by the permission of the waves and wind, to carry us about several of the Islands, with which he is acquainted enough to show us whatever curious is given by Nature or left by antiquity; but we grow afraid of deviating from our way home lest we should be shut up for months upon some little protuberance of earth, that just appears above the sea, and perhaps is scarcely marked upon a Map.

You remember the Doge of Genoa[17] who being asked what struck him most at the French Court, answered 'Myself'. I cannot think many things here more likely to affect the fancy, than to see Johnson ending his sixty fourth year in the wilderness of the Hebrides.

But now I am here, it will gratify me very little to return without seeing or doing my best to see what these places afford. I have a desire to instruct myself in the whole system of pastoral life, but I know not whether I shall be able to perfect the idea. However I have many pictures in my mind, which I could not have had without this Journey . . . I keep a book of remarks, and Boswel writes a regular journal of our travels, which, I think, contains as much of what I say and do, as of all other occurrences together—'For such a faithful Chronicler as Griffith'. . . .[18]

Oct. 3. The Wind is now changed, and if we snatch the moment of opportunity, an Escape from this Island is become practicable. I have no reason to complain of my reception, yet I long to be again at home. You and my Master may perhaps expect after this description of Skie, some account of myself. My eye is, I am afraid, not fully recovered, my ears are not mended, my nerves seem to grow weaker, and I have been otherwise not as well as I sometimes am, but think myself lately better. This Climate perhaps is not within my degrees of healthy Latitude.

Thus have I given my most honoured Mistress the story of me and my little ramble. We are now going to some other Isle, to what we know not, the Wind will tell us.

I am Madam
Your most humble Servant
Sam: Johnson

Compliments to Queeney and Jack and Lucy and all.

[17] Properly Venice.
[18] "He said to-day, while reading my Journal, 'This will be a great treasure to us some years hence.'" Johnson's notebook has not been found. The quotation is from Shakespeare's *Henry VIII*, slightly altered.

106. To Henry Thrale

Isle of Mull, October 15, 1773

Dear Sir

Since I had the honour of writing to my mistress, we have been hindered from returning, by a tempest almost continual. We tried eight days ago to come hither, but were driven by the wind into the isle of *Col*, in which we were confined eight days.[19] We hired a sloop to bring us hither, and hope soon to get to Edinburgh. . . .

107. To Mrs. Thrale

Inveraray, October 23, 1773

Honoured Mistress

My last letters to you and my dear Master were written from Mull, the third Island of the Hebrides in extent; there is no post, and I took the opportunity of a Gentlemans passage to the main Land.

Oct. 16. In Mull we were confined two days by the weather; on the third We got on horseback, and after a journey difficult and tedious over rocks naked and valleys untracked, through a country of barrenness and solitude, we came almost in the dark to seaside, weary and dejected having met with nothing but water falling from the mountains that could raise any image of delight. Our company was the young Laird of Coll and his servant. Coll made every Maclean open his house and supply us with horses when we departed. But the horses of this country are small, and I was not mounted to my wish.[20]

[19] The violent passage from Skye to Coll was the travelers' most dangerous experience. "I now saw what I never saw before, a prodigious sea, with immense billows coming upon a vessel, so as that it seemed hardly possible to escape. There was something grandly horrible in the sight." (Boswell's *Tour*.) Johnson stayed below the whole trip.

[20] "Here I first mounted a little highland steed, and if there had been many spectators, should have been somewhat ashamed of my figure in the march. . . . A bulky man upon one of their backs makes a very disproportionate appearance." (*Journey*.) "I said to Dr. Johnson, 'I wish, Sir, *the club* saw you in this attitude.'" (Boswell's *Tour*.)

At the seaside we found the ferry boat departed, if it had been where it was expected, the wind was against us, and the hour was late, nor was it very desirable to cross the sea in darkness with a small boat. The Captain of a sloop that had been driven thither by the storms, saw our distress and as we were hesitating and deliberating sent his boat, which by Coll's order, transported us to the Isle of *Ulva;* We were introduced to Mr Macquarry, the head of a small Clan, whose ancestors have reigned in Ulva beyond Memory, but who has reduced himself by his negligence and folly to the necessity of selling this venerable patrimony.

On the next morning Oct. 17 We passed the strait to *Inch Kenneth* an Island about a mile in length, and less than half a mile broad, in which Kenneth a Scottish Saint established a small clerical college of which the Chapell walls are still standing. At this place I beheld a scene which I wish you and my Master and Queeney had partaken. The only family on the Island is that of Sir Allan the chief of the ancient and numerous clan of Maclean, the clan which claims the second place, yielding only to Macdonald, in the line of Battle. Sir Allan, a Chieftain, a Baronet, and a soldier, inhabits in this insulated desart, a thatched hut with no chambers. Young Coll, who owns him as his chief and whose Cousin was his Lady, had, I believe, given him some notice of our visit. He received us with the Soldier's frankness, and the Gentleman's elegance, and introduced us to his daughters, two young Ladies who have not wanted Education suitable to their birth, and who in their cottage neither forgot their dignity, nor affected to remember it.

Do not you wish to have been with us?

Sir Allan's affairs are in disorder, by the fault of his ancestors, and while he forms some scheme for retrieving them, he has retreated hither. When our Salutations were over he showed us the Island. We walked uncovered into the chapel, and saw in the reverend ruin, the effects of precipitate reformation. The floor is covered with ancient gravestones of which the inscriptions are not now legible, and without some of the chief families still continue the right of Sepulture. The altar is not yet quite demolished, beside it on the right side is a Bas relief of the Virgin with her Child, and an Angel hovering over her, on the other side still stands a hand bell, which though it has no clapper neither presbyterian bigotry, nor barbarian wantoness has yet taken away. The Chappel is about thirty eight feet long, and eighteen broad. Boswel, who is very pious, went into it at night to perform his devotions, but came back in haste for fear of Spectres.[21]

Near the chappel is a fountain to which the water, remarkably pure, is conveyed from a distant hill through pipes laid by the Romish Clergy, which still perform the office of conveyance, though they have never been repaired since Popery was suppressed.

We soon after went into dinner, and wanted neither the comforts nor the elegancies of life. There were several dishes, and variety of liquours. The servants live in another cottage, in which I suppose the meat is drest.

Towards evening Sir Allan told us, that Sunday never passed over him like another day. One of the Ladies read, and read very well, the Evening services—And Paradise was open'd in the wild.[22]

Next day 18. We went and wandered among the rocks on the shore, while the boat was busy in catching oysters, of which there is a great bed. Oysters lye upon the sand one, I think, sticking to another, and Cockles are found a few inches under the sand. We then went into the boat to *Sondiland* a little Island, very near. We found it a wild rock of about ten acres, part naked, part covered with sand, out of which we picked shells, and part cloathed with a thin layer of mould on the grass of which a few sheep are sometimes fed. We then came back and dined. I passed part of the Afternoon in reading, and in the evening one of the Ladies played on her harpsichord, and I believe Boswel danced with the other.

On the 19th We persuaded Sir Allan to launch his boat again, and go with us to Icolmkil,[23] where the first great Preacher of Christianity to the Scots[24] built a Church, and settled a Monastry. In our way we stopped to examine a very uncommon Cave on the coast of

[21] "I indulged my inclination to what is called superstitious prayer. . . . I felt a kind of pleasing awful confusion. I was for going into the chapel, but a tremor seized me for ghosts, and I hastened back to the house." (Boswell's *Tour*, 1936 Manuscript edition.)

[22] Pope, "Eloisa to Abelard."

[23] Iona.

[24] St. Columba.

Mull. We had some difficulty to make our way over the vast masses of broken rocks that lye before the entrance, and at the mouth were embarrassed with stones which the sea had accumulated as at Brighthelmston, but as we advanced we reached a floor of soft sand, and as we left the light behind us, walked along a very spacious cavity vaulted over head with an arch almost regular, by which a mountain was sustained, at least a very lofty rock. From this magnificent cavern, went a narrow passage to the right hand, which we entered with a candle, and though it was obstructed with great stones, clambered over them to a second expansion of the Cave, in which there lies a great square stone which might serve as a table. The air here was very warm but not oppressive, the flame of the candle continued pyramidal.[25] The cave goes onward to an unknown extent, but we were now 160 yards underground; we had but one Candle, and had never heard of any that went further and came back. We therefore thought it prudent to return.

Going forward we came to a cluster of rocks black and horrid which Sir Allan chose for the place where he would eat his dinner. We climbed till we got seats. The stores were opened and the repast taken.

We then entered the boat again, the night came upon us, the wind rose, the sea swelled, and Boswel desired to be set on dry ground. We however persued our navigation, and passed by several little Islands in the silent solemnity of faint moonshine, seeing little, and hearing only the wind and the water.[26] At last we reached the Island, the venerable seat of ancient sanctity, where secret piety reposed, and where fallen greatness was reposited. The Island has no house of entertainment, and we manfully made our bed in a Farmers Barn.

The Description I hope to give you another time.

> I am, Madam,
>
> Your most obedient and most humble servant
>
> *Sam: Johnson*

[25] A sign that the air was pure.

[26] "As we sailed along by moon-light, in a sea somewhat rough, and often between black and gloomy rocks, Dr. Johnson said, 'If this be not *roving among the Hebrides*, nothing is.'" (Boswell's *Tour.*)

108. To Henry Thrale

Inveraray, October 23, 1773

Dear Sir

We have gotten at last out of the Hebrides; some account of our travels I have sent to my Mistress, and I have inclosed an ode which I wrote in the Isle of Skie . . .

Yesterday we landed, and to day came hither. We purpose to visit Auchenleck, the seat of Mr Boswel's Father, then to pass a day at Glasgow, and return to Edinburgh.

About ten miles of this days journey were uncommonly amusing. We travelled with very little light, in a storm of wind and rain, we passed about fifty five streams that crossed our way, and fell into a river that for a very great part of our road, foamed and roared beside us, all the rougher powers of Nature, except thunder were in motion, but there was no danger. I should have been sorry to have missed any of the inconveniences, to have had more light, or less rain, for their cooperation crowded the scene, and filled the mind. . . .[27]

109. To James Boswell, Edinburgh

November 27, 1773

Dear Sir

I came home last night, without any incommodity, danger, or weariness, and am ready to begin a new journey. I shall go to Oxford on Monday. I know Mrs. Boswell wished me well to go;[28] her wishes have not been disappointed. Mrs. Williams has received Sir A's letter.

Make my compliments to all those to whom my compliments may be welcome.

[27] "The wind was loud, the rain was heavy, and the whistling of the blast, the fall of the shower, the rush of the cataracts, and the roar of the torrent, made a nobler chorus of the rough musick of nature than it had ever been my chance to hear before." (*Journey.*)

[28] This is the first of many references to Mrs. Boswell's not entirely fictional animosity.

Let the box be sent as soon as it can, and let me know when to expect it.[29]

Enquire, if you can, the order of the Clans: Macdonald is first, Maclean second; further I cannot go. Quicken Dr. Webster.[30]

> I am, Sir,
> Yours affectionately
> *Sam. Johnson*

110. To John Taylor, Ashbourne

January 15, 1774

Dear Sir

When I was at Edinburgh I had a letter from you, telling me that in answer to some enquiry you were informed that I was in the Sky. I was then I suppose in the western Islands of Scotland; I set out on the northern expedition August 6, and came back to Fleet Street, November 26. I have seen a new region.

I have been upon seven of the Islands, and probably should have visited many more, had we not begun our journey so late in the year, that the stormy weather came upon us, and the storms have I believe for about five months hardly any intermission.

Your Letter told me you were better. When you write do not forget to confirm that account. I had very little ill health while I was on the journey, and bore rain and wind tolerably well. I had a cold and deafness only for a few days, and those days I passed at a good house. I have traversed the east coast of Scotland from south to north from Edinburgh to Inverness, and the west coast from north to south, from the Highlands to Glasgow, and am come back, as I went,

> Sir
> Your affectionate humble servant
> *Sam: Johnson*

[29] "This was a box containing a number of curious things which he had picked up in Scotland, particularly some horn spoons." (Boswell, *Life of Johnson*.)

[30] There was no settled order, Boswell told him. Dr. Webster of Edinburgh had promised him some information.

February 1774-August 1775

Johnson was off again with the Thrales for a visit to western England and Wales before his Journey *was even through the press, but the tour to the Hebrides had marked a peak of almost untempered pleasure he was never again to attain. He looks back to it often with nostalgia in the downhill years. "The expedition to the Hebrides was the most pleasant journey that I ever made. Such an effort annually would give the world a little diversification." (1776) "Our ramble in the islands hangs upon my imagination. I can hardly help imagining that we shall go again." (1777) "Shall we ever have another frolick like our Journey to the Hebrides?" (1782)*

He was unimpressed, for the most part, by the castles, churches, country homes, and scenery of Wales. His annual ramble to the country was a bore. Oxford conservatively added its doctoral degree to Dublin's at Lord North's recommendation, and Boswell was down at Easter-time for more talk, and more shorthand notes.

The year was most notably diversified by two private battles, both recorded in the letters: the engagement with James Macpherson (and with Scotsmen generally) brought on by the cannonades of his Journey; *and a pamphlet-war with the Patriots, occasioned by Johnson's anti-American tracts. War with the Americans had broken out in April, but Johnson had long since taken sides with King George.*

111. To James Boswell, Edinburgh

Streatham, June 21, 1774

Dear Sir

Yesterday I put the first sheets of the 'Journey to the Hebrides' to the press. I have endeavoured to do you some justice in the first paragraph. It will be one volume in octavo, not thick.

It will be proper to make some presents in Scotland. You shall tell me to whom I shall give; and I have stipulated twenty five for you to give in your own name. Some will take the present better from me, others better from you. In this, you who are to live in the place ought to direct. Consider it. Whatever you can get for my purpose, send me; and make my compliments to your lady and both the young ones.

I am, Sir, your, &c.,
Sam. Johnson.

112. To James Boswell, Edinburgh

July 4, 1774

Dear Sir . . .

Of poor dear Dr. Goldsmith there is little to be told, more than the papers have made publick. He died of a fever, made, I am afraid, more violent by uneasiness of mind. His debts began to be heavy, and all his resources were exhausted. Sir Joshua is of opinion that he owed not less than two thousand pounds. Was ever poet so trusted before? . . .

113. To Bennet Langton, Langton

July 5, 1774

Dear Sir

You have reason to reproach me that I have left your last letter so long unanswered, but I had nothing particular to say. Chambers you find, is gone far, and poor Goldsmith is gone much further. He died of a fever exasperated, as I believe, by the fear of distress. He had raised money and squandred it, by every artifice of acquisition and folly of expence. But let not his frailties be remembred; he was a very great Man.

I have just begun to print my Journey to the Hebrides and am leaving the press to take another journey into Wales, whither Mr. Thrale is going, to take possession of at least five hundred a year, fallen to his Lady. All at Streatham that are alive are well.

I have never recovered from the last dreadful Ilness but flatter myself that I grow gradually better; much however yet remains to mend. Κύριε ἐλέησον.¹

If you have the Latin version of *Busy, curious, thirsty fly*, be so kind as to transcribe and send it, but you need not be in haste, for I shall be I know not where, for at least five weeks. I wrote the following tetrastick on poor Goldsmith.

> Τὸν τάφον εἰσοράας τὸν Ὀλιβαρίοιο, κονίην
> Ἄφροσι μὴ σεμνὴν, Ξεῖνε, πόδεσσι πάτει·
> Οἷσι μέμηλε φύσις, μέτρων χάρις, ἔργα παλαιῶν,
> Κλαίετε ποιήτην, ἱστόρικον, φύσικον.²

Please to make my most respectful compliments to all the Ladies, and remember me to young George, and his sister. I reckon George begins to show a pair of heels.

Do not be sullen now, but let me find a letter when I come back.

I am Dear Sir,
Your affectionate humble Servant,
Sam: Johnson

---

¹ "Lord, have mercy on us."
² As translated by William Seward,

> Whoe'er thou art, with reverence tread
> Where Goldsmith's letter'd dust is laid.
> If nature and the historic page,
> If the sweet muse thy care engage,
> Lament him dead, whose powerful mind
> Their various energies combin'd.

114. To James Boswell, Edinburgh

October 1, 1774

Dear Sir

Yesterday I returned from my Welch journey. I was sorry to leave my book suspended so long; but having an opportunity of seeing, with so much convenience, a new part of the island, I could not reject it. I have been in five of the six counties of North Wales; and have seen St. Asaph and Bangor, the two seats of their bishops; have been upon Penmanmaur and Snowden,[3] and passed over into Anglesea. But Wales is so little different from England, that it offers nothing to the speculation of the traveller. . . .

115. To James Boswell, Edinburgh

November 26, 1774

Dear Sir

Last night I corrected the last page of our 'Journey to the Hebrides'. The printer has detained it all this time, for I had, before I went into Wales, written all except two sheets. 'The Patriot'[4] was called for by my political friends on Friday, was written on Saturday, and I have heard little of it. So vague are conjectures at a distance. As soon as I can, I will take care that copies be sent to you, for I would wish that they might be given before they are bought; but I am afraid that Mr. Strahan will send to you and to the booksellers at the same time. Trade is as diligent as courtesy. I have mentioned all that you recommended. Pray make my compliments to Mrs. Boswell and the younglings. The club has, I think, not yet met.

Tell me, and tell me honestly, what you think and what others say of our travels. Shall we touch the continent?

I am, dear Sir,

Your most humble servant,

Sam. Johnson

[3] Mountains in Northern Wales.

[4] A bitterly ironic Tory pamphlet reviling Johnson's enemies, the demagogues and the democrats who "arrogate to themselves the name of Patriots."

116. *To William Strahan*

November 30, 1774

Sir

I waited on you this morning having forgotten your new engagement;[5] for this you must not reproach me, for if I had looked upon your present station with malignity, I could not have forgotten it.

I came to consult you upon a little matter that gives me some uneasiness. In one of the pages there is a severe censure of the Clergy of an English Cathedral which I am afraid is just, but I have since recollected that from me it may be thought improper for the Dean did me a kindness about forty years ago. He is now very old, and I am not young. Reproach can do him no good, and in myself I know not whether it is zeal or wantonness.[6]

Can a leaf be cancelled without too much trouble? Tell me what I shall do. I have no settled choice, but I would not refuse to allow the charge. To cancel it seems the surer side. Determine for me.

I am, Sir,

Your most humble servant

Sam: Johnson

Tell me your mind, if you will cancel it, I will write something to fill up the vacuum. Please to direct to the Borough.[7]

117. *To John Hollyer*

December 6, 1774

Sir,

I take the liberty of writing to You with whom I have no acquaintance and whom I have therefore very little right to trouble,

[5] Strahan had just been elected to Parliament.

[6] In his discussion of the denudation of Elgin Cathedral in Scotland, Johnson had originally written, "There is now, as I have heard, a body of men, not less decent or virtuous than the Scotish council, longing to melt the lead of an English cathedral. What they shall melt, it were just that they should swallow." The men were the Dean and chapter of Lichfield Cathedral in Johnson's native city.

[7] I.e., the Thrales' house in Southwark.

but as it is about a man equally or almost equally related to both of us, I hope You will excuse it.

I have lately received a letter from our Cousin Thomas Johnson complaining of great distress. His distress I suppose is real, but how can it be prevented. In 1772 about Christmas I sent him thirty pounds, because he thought he could do something in a shop; many have lived who began with less. In the Summer 1773 I sent him ten pounds more, as I had promised him. What was the event? In the Spring 1774 he wrote me word that he was in debt for rent, and in want of clothes. That is, he had in about sixteen months consumed forty pounds, and then writes for more without any mention of either misconduct or misfortune. This seems to me very strange, and I shall be obliged to you if you can inform me, or make him inform me how the money was spent, and give me your advice what can be done for him with prudence and efficacy.

He is, I am afraid, not over sensible of the impropriety of his management, for he came to visit me in the Summer. I was in the country which perhaps was well for us both; I might have used him harshly, and then have repented.

I have sent a bill for five pounds which you will be so kind to get discounted for him, and see the money properly applyed, and give me your advice what can be done.

I am Sir

Your humble Servant

Sam: Johnson

118. To Dr. William Hunter

December 29, 1774

Sir

I am very much obliged by your willingness to present my book[8] to His Majesty. I have not courage to offer it myself, yet I cannot forbear to wish that He may see it, because it endeavours to describe a part of his Subjects, seldom visited, and little known, and his Benevolence will not despise the meanest of his people.

[8] The *Journey to the Western Islands.*

I have sent you a book, to which you are very justly entitled, and beg that it may be admitted to stand in your library however little it may add to its elegance or dignity.

I am, Sir,

Your most humble Servant,

Sam: Johnson

119. To Mrs. Thrale

December 1774

Madam

You must not tell any body but Mr Thrale that the King fell to reading the book as soon as he got it, when any thing struck him, he read aloud to the Queen, and the Queen would not stay to get the King's book, but borrowed Dr Hunter's. See now. Of the two Queens[9] who has the better tast?

Of all this you must absolutely say nothing to any body.

120. To James Macpherson[10]

January 20, 1775

Mr James Macpherson—I received your foolish and impudent note. Whatever insult is offered me I will do my best to repel, and what I cannot do for myself the law will do for me. I will not desist from

[9] The other is, presumably, Mrs. Thrale.

[10] James Macpherson published, in 1760-63, several fragments of un-rhymed rhapsodic verse (the "Ossian" poems) which he claimed to have translated from ancient Gaelic manuscripts—manuscripts which he never produced. Despite the extraordinary Ossian vogue that swept Europe thereafter ("the Scottish Homer," "Shakespeare and Ossian"), Johnson consistently refused to acknowledge the worth or the authenticity of the work. In his *Journey*, in 1774, he announced his disbelief explicitly, and impugned Macpherson's integrity in no uncertain terms. Macpherson demanded that Johnson cancel the injurious expressions, with public apology. Johnson refused. The Scotsman then challenged him more directly. Undaunted, Johnson armed himself with "an oak-plant of a tremendous size," and sent one of his most famous letters. (Johnson's fuller view of the issue is summarized in Letter 122.)

Mr James Macpherson — I received your bright and impudent note. Whatever injury is offered me I will do my best to repel, and what I cannot do for my self the law will do for me. I will not desist from declaring what I think a cheat from my fear of the menaces of a ruffian.

You want me to retract. What shall I retract? I thought your book an imposture from the beginning. I think it upon your surer warrant an imposture still. For this opinion I give the publick my reasons which I here dare you to refute.

But however I may despise you, I reverence truth
and if you can prove the genuineness of the work
I will confess it. You may carp I confess, your abilities
since your Homer are not so formidable, and that I
have heard of your morals disposes me to pay regard
not to what you shall say, but to what you can prove.

You may print this if you will.

Sam: Johnson
Jan. 20. 1775

detecting what I think a cheat, from any fear of the menaces of a Ruffian.

You want me to retract. What shall I retract? I thought your book an imposture from the beginning, I think it upon yet surer reasons an imposture still. For this opinion I give the publick my reasons which I here dare you to refute.

But however I may despise you, I reverence truth and if you can prove the genuineness of the work I will confess it. Your rage I defy, your abilities since your Homer[11] are not so formidable, and what I have heard of your morals disposes me to pay regard not to what you shall say, but to what you can prove.

You may print this if you will.

Sam: Johnson

121. *To James Boswell, Edinburgh*

January 21, 1775

Dear Sir,

I long to hear how you like the book; it is, I think, much liked here. But Macpherson is very furious; can you give me any more intelligence about him, or his Fingal? Do what you can, and do it quickly. Is Lord Hailes on our side?

Pray let me know what I owed you when I left you, that I may send it to you.

I am going to write about the Americans.[12] If you have picked up any hints among your lawyers, who are great masters of the law of nations, or if your own mind suggests any thing, let me know. But mum,—it is a secret.

I will send your parcel of books as soon as I can; but I cannot do as I wish. However, you find every thing mentioned in the book which you recommended.

Langton is here; we are all that ever we were. He is a worthy fellow, without malice, though not without resentment.

[11] Macpherson's "Ossianic" translation of the *Iliad* in 1773 was a notable failure.
[12] *Taxation No Tyranny* (1775) was to be Johnson's most famous anti-American outburst.

Poor Beauclerk is so ill, that his life is thought to be in danger. Lady Di. nurses him with very great assiduity.

Reynolds has taken too much to strong liquor, and seems to delight in his new character. . . .

122. *To James Boswell, Edinburgh*

February 7, 1775

My dear Boswell,

I am surprized that, knowing as you do the disposition of your countrymen to tell lies in favour of each other, you can be at all affected by any reports that circulate among them. Macpherson never in his life offered me the sight of any original or of any evidence of any kind, but thought only of intimidating me by noise and threats, till my last answer,—that I would not be deterred from detecting what I thought a cheat, by the menaces of a ruffian,—put an end to our correspondence.

The state of the question is this. He, and Dr. Blair, whom I consider as deceived, say, that he copied the poem from old manuscripts. His copies, if he had them, and I believe him to have none, are nothing. Where are the manuscripts? They can be shown if they exist, but they were never shown. *De non existentibus et non apparentibus,* says our law, *eadem est ratio.*[13] No man has a claim to credit upon his own word, when better evidence, if he had it, may be easily produced. But, so far as we can find, the Erse language was never written till very lately for the purposes of religion. A nation that cannot write, or a language that was never written, has no manuscripts.

But whatever he has, he never offered to show. If old manuscripts should now be mentioned, I should, unless there were more evidence than can be easily had, suppose them another proof of Scotch conspiracy in national falsehood.

Do not censure the expression; you know it to be true. . . .

[13] "What cannot be produced must be treated as non-existent."

123. To William Strahan

Oxford, March 1, 1775

Sir

I am sorry to see that all the alterations proposed [14] are evidence of timidity. You may be sure that I do not wish to publish, what those for whom I write do not like to have published. But print me half a dozen copies in the original state, and lay them up for me. It concludes well enough as it is.

When you print it, if you print it, please to frank one to me here, and frank another to Mrs Aston as Stow Hill, Lichfield.

The changes are not for the better, except where the facts were mistaken. The last paragraph was indeed rather contemptuous, there was once more of it which I put out myself.[15]

I am Sir

Your humble Servant

Sam: Johnson

124. To Mrs. Thrale

April 1, 1775

Madam . . .

The other Oxford news is, that they have sent me a degree of Doctor of Laws, with such praises in the diploma, as, perhaps, ought to make me ashamed; they are very like your praises. I wonder whether I shall ever show them to you. . . .

[14] In *Taxation No Tyranny.*
[15] The conclusion had originally contained a gross and gratuitous insult to Lord Chatham.

125. *To Thomas Fothergill, Oxford*

April 7, 1775

Viro Reverendo Thomae Fothergill, S.T.P. Universitatis
Oxoniensis Vice-Cancellario.

S.P.D.
Sam. Johnson.

Multis non est opus, ut testimonium quo, te praeside, Oxonienses
nomen meum posteris commendârunt, quali animo acceperim com-
pertum faciam. Nemo sibi placens non laetatur; nemo sibi non placet,
qui vobis, literarum arbitris, placere potuit. Hoc tamen habet incom-
modi tantum beneficium, quod mihi nunquam posthàc sine vestrae
famae detrimento vel labi liceat vel cessare; semperque sit timendum,
ne quod mihi tam eximiae laudi est, vobis aliquando fiat opprobrio.
Vale.[16]

126. *To John Taylor, Ashbourne*

April 8, 1775

Dear Sir

When shall I come down to you? I believe I can get away pretty
early in May, if you have any mind of me; If you have none, I can
move in some other direction. So tell me what I shall do. . . .

The patriots pelt me with answers. Four pamflets I think, already,
besides newspapers and reviews, have been discharged against me.
I have tried to read two of them, but did not go through them.

Now and then I call on Congreve, though I have little or no rea-

---

[16] Johnson's degree was granted on March 30. Dr. Chapman's translation is:

> I need not use many words to tell you how I receive the com-
> mendation with which the University over which you preside has
> transmitted my name to posterity. Every man is glad to think well of
> himself; and that man must think well of himself, of whom you, the
> arbiters of letters, can think well. But the good you have done me has
> one drawback: henceforth any fault of mine, of commission or omis-
> sion, will hurt your reputation; I must always fear that what is a signal
> honour to me may one day bring discredit upon you.

son to think that he wants or wishes to see me. I sometimes dispute with him, but I think he has not studied. He has really ill health, and seems to have given way to that indulgence which sickness is always in too much haste to claim. He confesses a bottle aday.

I am Sir
Your humble Servant
Sam: Johnson

127. To Bennet Langton

May 21, 1775

Dear Sir

I have an old Amanuensis in great distress. I have given what I think I can give, and begged till I cannot tell where to beg again. I put into his hands this morning four guineas. If you could collect three guineas more, it would clear him from his present difficulty.

I am, Sir,
Your most humble Servant,
Sam: Johnson.

128. To Mrs. Thrale

Lichfield, June 11, 1775

Dearest Lady . . .

You never told me, and I omitted to enquire, how you were entertained by Boswell's Journal. One would think the man had been hired to be a spy upon me. He was very diligent, and caught opportunities of writing from time to time. You may now conceive yourself tolerably well acquainted with the expedition. Folks want me to go to Italy, but I say you are not for it. However write often to,

Madam, Your, &c.

129. To Mrs. Thrale

Lichfield, June 19, 1775

Dear Madam . . .

Lady Smith has got a new postchaise, which is not nothing to talk on at Lichfield. Little things here serve for conversation. Mrs

Aston's Parrot pecked my leg, and I heard of it some time after at Mrs Cobb's.

> —We deal in nicer things
> Than routing armies, and dethroning kings.

a week ago Mrs Cobb gave me sweetmeats to breakfast, and I heard of it last night at Stowhill.
If you are for small talk.

> —Come on, and do the best you can
> I fear not you, nor yet a better man.

I could tell you about Lucy's two cats, and Brill her brother's old dog, who is gone deaf, but the day would fail me. Suadentque cadentia sidera somnum.[17] So said Aeneas but I have not yet had my diner. I have begun early for what would become of the nation if a Letter of this importance should miss the post? Pray write to
Dear Madam
Your most obedient and most humble Servant
Sam: Johnson

130. To Mrs. Thrale

Lichfield, June 23, 1775
Dear Madam
So now you have been at the regatta, for I hope you got tickets somewhere, else you wanted me, and I shall not be sorry, because you fancy You can do so well without me, but however I hope you got tickets, and were dressed fine and fanciful, and made a fine part of the fine show, and heard musick, and said good things, and staid on the water four hours after midnight, and came well home, and slept, and dreamed of the regatta, and waked, and found yourself in bed, and thought now it is all over, only I must write about it to Lichfield.

We make a hard shift here to live on without a regatta. The cherries are ripe at Stowhil, and the currants are ripening, and the Ladies are very kind to me. . . .

---

[17] "And setting stars invite to rest." (Virgil.)

131

131. To Mrs. Thrale

Ashbourne, July 11, 1775

Dear Madam . . .

Dr. Taylor wants to be gardening. He means to buy a piece of ground in the neighbourhood, and surround it with a wall, and build a gardener's house upon it, and have fruit, and be happy. Much happiness it will not bring him; but what can he do better? If I had money enough, what would I do? Perhaps, if you and master did not hold me, I might go to Cairo, and down the Red Sea to Bengal, and take a ramble in India. Would this be better than building and planting? It would surely give more variety to the eye, and more amplitude to the mind. Half fourteen thousand would send me out to see other forms of existence, and bring me back to describe them. . . .

132. To Mrs. Thrale

Lichfield, August 1, 1775

Dear Madam . . .

America now fills every mouth, and some heads; and a little of it shall come into my letter. I do not much like the news. Our troops have indeed the superiority, five and twenty hundred have driven five thousand from their intrenchment but the Americans fought skilfully;[18] had coolness enough in the battle to carry off their men; and seem to have retreated orderly for they were not persued. They want nothing but confidence in their leaders and familiarity with danger. Our business is to persue their main army, and disperse it by a decisive battle and then waste the country till they sue for peace. If we make war by parties and detachments, dislodge them from one place, and exclude them from another, we shall by a local, gradual, and ineffectual war, teach them our own knowledge, harden their obstinacy, and strengthen their confidence, and at last come to fight on equal terms of skill and bravery, without equal numbers. . . .

[18] That is, at the battle of Bunker Hill, June 17. Although victorious in the battle, the King's forces under Howe suffered over 1000 casualties at colonial hands.

133. To James Boswell, Edinburgh

August 27, 1775

Dear Sir,

I am now returned from the annual ramble into the middle counties. Having seen nothing that I had not seen before, I have nothing to relate. Time has left that part of the island few antiquities; and commerce has left the people no singularities. I was glad to go abroad, and, perhaps, glad to come home; which is, in other words, I was, I am afraid, weary of being at home, and weary of being abroad. Is not this the state of life? But, if we confess this weariness, let us not lament it; for all the wise and all the good say, that we may cure it. . . .

Never, my dear Sir, do you take it into your head that I do not love you; you may settle yourself in full confidence both of my love and my esteem; I love you as a kind man, I value you as a worthy man, and hope in time to reverence you as a man of exemplary piety. I hold you as Hamlet has it, 'in my heart of heart', and therefore, it is little to say, that I am,

Sir,
Your affectionate humble servant,
Sam. Johnson

September 1775-June 1777

Another voyage begins the next period—a two-month journey to France with the Thrales in the fall of 1775. "Fixed to a spot when I was young," he wrote Taylor, "and roving the world when others are contriving to sit still, I am wholly unsettled." Johnson noted in his travel diary scores of Gallic details; but he remained, for the most part, very much the stolid English tourist, seeing little for all that he saw. The Scottish adventure could not be recaptured; he would write no Journey to Paris. *"As I entered [the Palais Bourbon], my wife was in my mind: She would have been pleased. Having nobody to please, I am little pleased."*

Boswell came down again in March 1776, to join Johnson on the Midlands circuit: but at Lichfield, on April 25, the tour was cut short by word of the sudden death of young Harry, the Thrales' only surviving son. "A total extinction of their family," Johnson called it; "I would have gone to the extremity of the earth to have preserved this boy." He had reason to lament, more reason than he knew: his Italian tour was cancelled; his patron, bereft of his heir, saddened into death; and finally the widow, once Johnson's surest ally, drifted away, and left him alone. The solitary, Thrale-less gloom of Johnson's dying years begins with the death of young Harry.

Johnson came home in haste at the news, to find Mrs. Thrale flying to Bath, where he followed the next month. His return to London in May was marked by the epic encounter with John Wilkes, his polar opposite in the political world, an affair stage-managed with all of Boswell's unparalleled gall.

He was crippled for the summer by a fitful return of the gout; September and October he passed, bored, at Brighton; January saw him in the grip of a suffocating asthma. He was doing nothing, he sometimes felt, but aging: even his mind, perhaps, was going:

> When I survey my past life, I discover nothing but a barren waste of time with some disorders of body, and disturbances of the mind very near to madness. . . .
>
> Days and months pass in a dream, and I am afraid that my memory grows less tenacious, and my observation less attentive. If I am decaying it is time to make haste.

(Diary, 1777)

On May 3, he wrote to Boswell, "I am engaged to write little Lives, and little Prefaces, to a little edition of the English Poets." The little Lives and little Prefaces, written over the next three years out of the wisdom of a lifetime, were to become his most famous and valuable work. The fact that he alone was considered for the task, as he alone had been considered for the Dictionary, is proof of his continuing dominion, active or dormant, over the world of English letters. The mind was not gone yet.

134. *To Robert Levett*

Calais, September 18, 1775

Dear Sir

We are here in France, after a very pleasing passage of no more than six hours. I know not when I shall write again, and therefore I write now, though you cannot suppose that I have much to say. You have seen France yourself. From this place we are going to Rouen, and from Rouen to Paris, where Mr. Thrale designs to stay about five or six weeks. We have a regular recommendation to the English resident, so we shall not be taken for vagabonds. We think to go one way and return another, and see as much as we can. I will try to speak a little French; I tried hitherto but little, but I spoke sometimes. If I heard better, I suppose I should learn faster.

I am, Sir,
Your humble servant,
Sam. Johnson.

135. *To Robert Levett*

Paris, October 22, 1775

Dear Sir

We are still here, commonly very busy in looking about us. We have been to day at Versailles. You have seen it, and I shall not describe it. We came yesterday from Fontainbleau, where the Court is now. We went to see the King and Queen at dinner, and the Queen was so impressed by Miss,[1] that she sent one of the gentlemen to enquire who she was. I find all true that you have ever told me of Paris. Mr. Thrale is very liberal, and keeps us two coaches, and a very fine table; but I think our cookery very bad. Mrs. Thrale got into a convent of English nuns, and I talked with her through the grate, and I am very kindly used by the English Benedictine friars. But upon the whole I cannot make much acquaintance here, and though the churches, palaces, and some private houses are very magnificent, there is no very great pleasure after having seen many, in seeing more; at least the pleasure, whatever it be, must some time

[1] Queeney Thrale.

have an end, and we are beginning to think when we shall come home. Mr. Thrale calculates that as we left Streatham on the fifteenth of September, we shall see it again about the fifteenth of November.

I think I had not been on this side of the sea five days before I found a sensible improvement in my health. I ran a race in the rain this day, and beat Baretti. Baretti is a fine fellow, and speaks French, I think, quite as well as English.

Make my compliments to Mrs. Williams; and give my love to Francis, and tell my friends that I am not lost.

I am, dear Sir,

Your affectionate humble, &c.

Sam. Johnson.

136. *To John Wesley*

February 6, 1776

Sir

When I received your Commentary on the Bible I durst not at first flatter myself that I was to keep it, having so little claim to so valuable a present; and when Mrs. Hall informed me of your kindness, was hindered from time to time from returning you those thanks, which I now entreat you to accept.

I have thanks likewise to return you for the addition of your important suffrage to my argument on the American question. To have gained such a mind as yours, may justly confirm me in my own opinion. What effect my paper has had upon the publick, I know not; but I have no reason to be discouraged. The Lecturer was surely in the right, who, though he saw his audience slinking away, refused to quit the Chair, while Plato staid.

I am, Reverend Sir,

Your most humble servant,

Sam: Johnson.

137. *To James Boswell, Edinburgh*

March 5, 1776

Dear Sir,

I have not had your letter half an hour; as you lay so much weight upon my notions, I should think it not just to delay my answer.

I am very sorry that your melancholy should return, and should be sorry likewise if it could have no relief but from my company. My counsel you may have when you are pleased to require it; but of my company you cannot in the next month have much, for Mr. Thrale will take me to Italy, he says, on the first of April. . . . I know not but we may scour the country together, for I have a mind to see Oxford and Lichfield before I set out on this long journey. To this I can only add, that

I am, dear Sir,

Your most affectionate humble servant,

Sam: Johnson

138. *To Mrs. Thrale*

Lichfield, March 25, 1776

Dear Madam

This letter will not, I hope, reach you many days before me, in a distress which can be so little relieved, nothing remains for a friend but to come and partake it.[2]

Poor dear sweet little Boy. When I read the letter this day to Mrs Aston, she said 'such a death is the next to Translation'. Yet, however I may convince myself of this, the tears are in my eyes, and yet I could not love him as you loved him, nor reckon on him for a future comfort, as you and his Father reckoned upon him.

He is gone, and we are going. We could not have enjoyed him long, and shall not long be separated from him. He has probably escaped many such pangs as you are now feeling.

Nothing remains but that with humble confidence We resign ourselves to almighty Goodness, and fall down without irreverent mur-

[2] Little Harry Thrale, age nine, the only surviving son of twelve Thrale children, died suddenly on the afternoon of the 23rd.

murs before the Sovereign Distributer of good and evil, with hope
that though sorrow endureth for a night, yet joy may come in the
Morning.[3]

I have known you, Madam, too long to think that you want any
arguments for submission to the supreme will, nor can my consolation have any effect but that of showing that I wish to comfort you.
What can be done you must do for yourself. Remember first that
your Child is happy, and then, that he is safe not only from the ills
of this world, but from those more formidable dangers which ex-
tend their mischief to eternity. You have brought into the world
a rational Being, have seen him happy during the little life that has
been granted him, and can have no doubt but that his Happiness is
now permanent and immutable.

When you have obtained by Prayer such tranquillity as nature
will admit, force your attention, as you can, upon your accustomed
duties, and accustomed entertainments. You can do no more for our
dear Boy, but you must not therefore think less on those whom your
attention may make fitter for the place to which he is gone.

I am Dearest, dearest Madam

Your most affectionate humble servant,

Sam: Johnson

139. To Mrs. Thrale, Bath

April 1, 1776

Dearest Madam

When you were gone Mr Thrale soon sent me away. I came next
day, and was made to understand that when I was wanted I should
be sent for; and therefore I have not gone yesterday or to day, but
I will soon go again whether invited or not. . . .

[3] Psalm 30:5.

140. To Mrs. Thrale

April 9, 1776

Dear Madam

Mr Thrale's alteration of purpose is not weakness of resolution; it is a wise man's compliance with the change of things, and with the new duties which the change produces. Whoever expects me to be angry will be disappointed. I do not even grieve at the effect. I grieve only at the cause. . . .

I am very little disappointed. I was glad to go, to places of so much celebrity, but had promised to myself no raptures, nor much improvement. . . .[4]

141. To Mrs. Thrale, Bath

May 16, 1776

Dear Madam

This is my third letter, well—sure I shall have something to morrow. Our business stands still. The Doctor says I must not go; and yet my stay does him no good. His Solicitor says he is sick, but I suspect he is sullen. The Doctor in the mean time has his head as full as yours at an Election. Livings and preferments, as if he were in want with twenty children, run in his head.[5] But a man must have his head on something small or great.

For my part, I begin to settle and keep company with grave aldermen. I dined yesterday in the poultry with Mr. Alderman Wilkes,[6] and Mr. Alderman Lee, and Counsellor Lee, his Brother. There sat you the while, so sober, with your Woodwards and your

[4] Johnson was "philosophical" regarding the cancellation of the Italian trip, but obviously disappointed.
[5] Dr. Taylor was vicar of Market Bosworth, Preacher of Broadway Chapel, Westminster, Prebendary of Westminster, Rector of Lawford, Essex, Perpetual Curate of St. Botolph's, Aldersgate (till 1776), and, after 1784, Rector of St. Margaret's, Westminster. He had tried, in vain, for the Deaneries of Rochester and Lincoln.
[6] This is Johnson's only recorded reference in the letters to "the most famous of all dinner-parties." See Boswell's *Life* (May 15, 1776) for the full account. "The poultry," here, refers to a London street.

Harringtons and my Aunt and her turnspit, and when they were gone, you think by chance on Johnson what is he doing? What should he be doing? he is breaking jokes with Jack Wilkes upon the Scots. Such Madam, are the vicissitudes of things. And there was Mrs. Knowles the Quaker that workes the sutile pictures, who is a great admirer of your conversation. She saw you at Mr Shaw's, at the election time. She is a Staffordshire Woman, and I am to go and see her. Staffordshire is the nursery of art, where they grow up till they are transplanted to London.

Yet it is strange that I hear nothing from you. I hope you are not angry, or sick. Perhaps you are gone without me for spite to see places. That is natural enough, for evil is very natural, but I shall vex, unless it does you good.

Stevens seems to be connected with Tyrwhit in publishing Chatterton's poems; he came very anxiously to know the result of our enquiries, and though he says, he always thought them forged, is not quite pleased to find us so fully convinced.[7]

I have written to Manucci to find his own way, for the *Law's delay*[8] makes it difficult for me to guess when I shall be, able to be, otherwise than by my inclination,

Madam,
Your most humble Servant
Sam: Johnson

142. To Sir Joshua Reynolds

May 16, 1776

Dear Sir

I have been kept away from You, I know not well how, and of these vexatious hindrances I know not when there will be an end. I therefore send you the poor dear Doctor's[9] epitaph. Read it first

[7] Johnson refers to the poems of Thomas Chatterton of Bristol, "the marvellous boy," who died a suicide in 1770 at the age of 18. They were extraordinary (though patently false) forgeries of medieval ballads. Tyrwhitt, his editor, and Steevens seem both to have been duped for a while.

[8] From *Hamlet*. Johnson had planned to go with Manucci to Bath, but he was held up by Taylor's legal affairs.

[9] Goldsmith.

yourself, and if you then think it right, show it to the Club. I am, you know, willing enough to be corrected. If you think any thing much amiss, keep it to yourself, till we come together. I have sent two copies, but prefer the card. The dates must be settled by Dr Percy.

I am, Sir,

Your most humble Servant,

Sam: Johnson

143. To Margaret Boswell, Edinburgh

May 16, 1776

Madam,

You must not think me uncivil in omitting to answer the letter with which you favoured me some time ago. I imagined it to have been written without Mr. Boswell's knowledge, and therefore supposed the answer to require, what I could not find, a private conveyance.

The difference with Lord Auchinleck is now over;[10] and since young Alexander has appeared, I hope no more difficulties will arise among you; for I sincerely wish you all happy. Do not teach the young ones to dislike me, as you dislike me yourself; but let me at least have Veronica's kindness, because she is my acquaintance.

You will now have Mr. Boswell home; it is well that you have him, he has led a wild life. I have taken him to Lichfield, and he has followed Mr. Thrale to Bath. Pray take care of him, and tame him. The only thing in which I have the honour to agree with you is, in loving him; and while we are so much of a mind in a matter of so much importance, our other quarrels will, I hope, produce no great bitterness.

I am, Madam,

Your most humble servant,

Sam. Johnson.

[10] Boswell had for a long time been in his father's disfavor even more than usual. The reconciliation was not permanent.

144. To Robert Levett

Brighthelmston, October 21, 1776

Dear Sir

Having spent about six weeks at this place, we have at length resolved upon returning. I expect to see you all in Fleet-street on the 30th of this month.

I did not go into the sea till last Friday, but think to go most of this week, though I know not that it does me any good. My nights are very restless and tiresome, but I am otherwise well.

I have written word of my coming to Mrs. Williams. Remember me kindly to Francis and Betsy.

I am, Sir,
Your humble servant,
Sam: Johnson

145. To James Boswell, Edinburgh

November 16, 1776

Dear Sir . . .

I was some weeks this autumn at Brighthelmston. The place was very dull, and I was not well: the expedition to the Hebrides was the most pleasant journey that I ever made. Such an effort annually would give the world a little diversification. . . .

146. To John Perkins

April 4, 1777

Mr Johnson sends compliments to Mr Perkins, and though he believes this foolish newspaper to be false, yet desires to know when Mr Perkins heard of Mr Thrale, and what he can tell of the ground of the report.[11]

[11] A report of Thrale's death.

147. To Henry Thrale

April 9, 1777

Dear Sir

This is a letter of pure congratulation. I congratulate you,

1. That you are alive.[12]

2. That you have got my mistress fixed again after her excentricities.

3. That my mistress has added to her conquests the Prince of Castiglione.

4. That you will not be troubled with me till to-morrow, when I shall come with [Dr. Taylor.]

5. That [Dr. Taylor] will go away in the evening.

I am, &c.

148. To James Boswell, Edinburgh

May 3, 1777

Dear Sir,

The story of Mr. Thrale's death, as he had neither been sick nor in any other danger, made so little impression upon me, that I never thought about obviating its effects on any body else. It is supposed to have been produced by the English custom of making April fools, that is, of sending one another on some foolish errand on the first of April.

Tell Mrs. Boswell that I shall taste her marmalade cautiously at first, *Timeo Danaos et dona ferentes.*[13] Beware, says the Italian proverb, of a reconciled enemy. But when I find it does me no harm, I shall then receive it and be thankful for it, as a pledge of firm, and, I hope, of unalterable kindness. She is after all, a dear, dear lady.

Please to return Dr. Blair thanks for his sermons. The Scotch write English wonderfully well. . . .

[12] "We are authorised to assure our Readers, that the Paragraph concerning the Death of Henry Thrale Esq; has no Foundation in Truth." *The Public Advertiser*, April 5, 1777.

[13] "I fear the Greeks, even bearing gifts." (Virgil; a proverbial reference to the Trojan Horse.)

Your frequent visits to Auchinleck, and your short stay there are very laudable and very judicious. Your present concord with your father gives me great pleasure; it was all that you seemed to want. My health is very bad, and my nights are very unquiet. What can I do to mend them? I have for this summer nothing better in prospect than a journey into Staffordshire and Derbyshire, perhaps with Oxford and Birmingham in my way.

Make my compliments to Miss Veronica; I must leave it to *her* philosophy to comfort you for the loss of little David. You must remember, that to keep three out of four is more than your share. Mrs. Thrale has but four out of eleven.

I am engaged to write little Lives, and little Prefaces, to a little edition of the English Poets. I think I have persuaded the booksellers to insert something of Thomson, and if you could give me information about him, for the life which we have is very scanty, I should be glad.

I am, dear Sir,
Your most affectionate humble servant,
Sam: Johnson

149. To John Taylor, Ashbourne

May 19, 1777

Dear Sir

I am required by Mrs Thrale to solicite you to exert your interest, that she may have a ticket of admission to the entertainment at Devonshire house. Do for her what You can.

I continue to have very troublesome and tedious nights, which I do not perceive any change of place to make better or worse. This is indeed at present my chief malady, but this is very heavy.

My thoughts were to have been in Staffordshire before now. But who does what he designs?—My purpose is still to spend part of the Summer amongst you; and of that hope I have no particular reason to fear the disappointment.

Poor Dod was sentenced last week. It is a thing almost without example for a Clergyman of his rank to stand at the bar for a capital breach of morality. I am afraid he will suffer. The Clergy seem not to be his friends. The populace that was extremely clamorous against him, begin to pity him. The time that was gained by an objection which was never considered as having any force, was of great use, as it allowed the publick resentment to cool. To spare his life, and his life is all that ought to be spared, would be now rather popular than offensive. How little he thought six months ago of being what he now is.[14]

I am Sir &c
Sam: Johnson

150. To Charles Jenkinson

June 20, 1777

Sir,

Since the conviction and condemnation of Dr. Dodd, I have had, by the intervention of a friend, some intercourse with him, and I am sure I shall lose nothing in your opinion by tenderness and commiseration. Whatever be the crime, it is not easy to have any knowledge of the delinquent without a wish that his life may be spared, at least when no life has been taken away by him. I will, therefore, take the liberty of suggesting some reasons for which I wish this unhappy being to escape the utmost rigour of his sentence.

He is, so far as I can recollect, the first clergyman of our church who has suffered publick execution for immorality; and I know not whether it would not be more for the interest of religion to bury such an offender in the obscurity of perpetual exile, than to expose him in a cart, and on the gallows, to all who for any reason are enemies to the clergy.

The supreme power has, in all ages, paid some attention to the

[14] Dodd was arrested in May for forging a £4200 bond in the name of Lord Chesterfield (the nephew and successor of Johnson's "patron"). Forgery being at the time (and until 1834) a capital crime, Dodd was sentenced to death. For over a month attempts were made to win him a pardon. At the solicitation of many friends, Johnson wrote speeches, letters, and petitions for Dodd—even his Last Solemn Declaration—all to no avail. The King and the Lord Chief Justice (partly in order not to appear under the dictation of a London mob) refused to grant a pardon, and Dodd was executed on June 27.

voice of the people; and that voice does not least deserve to be heard, when it calls out for mercy. There is now a very general desire that Dodd's life should be spared. More is not wished; and, perhaps, this is not too much to be granted.

If you, Sir, have any opportunity of enforcing these reasons, you may, perhaps, think them worthy of consideration: but whatever you determine, I most respectfully intreat that you will be pleased to pardon for this intrusion,

Sir,

Your most obedient

And most humble servant,

Sam. Johnson

151. To Dr. William Dodd

June 22, 1777

Sir,

I must seriously enjoin you not to let it be at all known that I have written this Letter, and to return the Copy to Mr. Allen in a Cover to me. I hope, I need not tell you that I wish it Success.— But do not indulge Hope.—Tell nobody.

Sir,

May it not offend your Majesty, that the most miserable of men applies himself to your clemency, as his last hope and his last refuge; that your mercy is most earnestly and humbly implored by a clergyman, whom your Laws and Judges have condemned to the horrour and ignominy of a publick execution.

I confess the crime, and own the enormity of its consequences, and the danger of its example. Nor have I the confidence to petition for impunity; but humbly hope, that publick security may be established, without the spectacle of a clergyman dragged through the streets, to a death of infamy, amidst the derision of the profligate and profane; and that justice may be satisfied with irrevocable exile, perpetual disgrace, and hopeless penury.

My life, Sir, has not been useless to mankind. I have benefited many. But my offenses against God are numberless, and I have

148

had little time for repentance. Preserve me, Sir, by your prerogative of mercy, from the necessity of appearing unprepared at that tribunal, before which Kings and Subjects must stand at last together. Permit me to hide my guilt in some obscure corner of a foreign country, where, if I can ever attain confidence to hope that my prayers will be heard, they shall be poured with all the fervour of gratitude for the life and happiness of your Majesty. I am, Sir,

Your Majesty's, &c.[15]

152. To Edmund Allen

June 22, 1777

Dear Sir

There was mention made of sending Dr Dod's sermon to the great Officers of State. I opposed it, but have now altered my Mind. Nothing can do harm, let every thing therefore be tried. Let Mr Jenkinson have his letter wherever he be. Let the Sermon be sent to every Body, and to the King if it can be done. He is, I believe more likely to read it, and to regard it than his Ministers. Let Lord Dartmouth have it, and Lord North.

I am Sir your humble servant

Sam: Johnson

153. To the Countess of Harrington

June 25, 1777

Madam

That Humanity which disposed Your Ladyship to engage me in favour of Dr Dodd, will incline You to forgive me when I take the Liberty of soliciting Your Influence in Support of my Endeavours, which, I am afraid, will otherwise be ineffectual. What could be done by the Powers which fall to my Share, has been warmly and carefully performed. The Time is now come when high Rank and high Spirit must begin their Operations. Dodd must

[15] The text of Johnson's letter for Dodd is from Boswell's *Life* (Hill-Powell edition, III, 145).

die at last unless your Ladyship shall be pleased to represent to his Majesty how properly the Life of a Delinquent may be granted to the Petitions of that Society for the sake of which he is to be punished; that the greatest Princes have thought it the highest Part of their Praise to be easily flexible to the Side of Mercy; and that whether the Case be consider'd as political or moral, the joint Petition of Three and Twenty Thousand Supplicants, ought not to be rejected, when even after all that they desire is granted, the Offender is still to suffer perpetual Exile, perpetual Infamy, and perpetual Poverty.

I am, Madam,

      Yr Ladyship's Most obedient and most humble Servt.

Sam: Johnson

154. To Dr. William Dodd

June 26, 1777

Dear Sir,

That which is appointed to all men is now coming upon you. Outward circumstances, the eyes and the thoughts of men, are below the notice of an immortal being about to stand the trial for eternity, before the Supreme Judge of heaven and earth. Be comforted: your crime, morally or religiously considered, has no very deep dye of turpitude. It corrupted no man's principles; it attacked no man's life. It involved only a temporary and reparable injury. Of this, and of all other sins, you are earnestly to repent; and may God, who knoweth our frailty and desireth not our death, accept your repentence, for the sake of his Son Jesus Christ our Lord.

In requital of those well-intended offices which you are pleased so emphatically to acknowledge, let me beg that you make in your devotions one petition for my eternal welfare.

I am, dear Sir,

      Your affectionate servant,

Sam. Johnson.

155. *To James Boswell, Edinburgh*

June 28, 1777

Dear Sir, . . .

Poor Dodd was put to death yesterday, in opposition to the recommendation of the jury—the petition of the city of London —and a subsequent petition signed by three-and-twenty thousand hands. Surely the voice of the publick, when it calls so loudly, and calls only for mercy, ought to be heard.

The saying that was given me in the papers I never spoke; but I wrote many of his petitions, and some of his letters. He applied to me very often. He was, I am afraid, long flattered with hopes of life; but I had no part in the dreadful delusion; for as soon as the King had signed his sentence, I obtained from Mr. Chamier an account of the disposition of the court towards him, with a declaration that there was *no hope even of a respite.* This letter immediately was laid before Dodd; but he believed those whom he wished to be right, as it is thought, till within three days of his end. He died with pious composure and resolution. I have just seen the Ordinary that attended him. His Address to his fellow-convicts offended the Methodists; but he had a Moravian with him much of his time. His moral character is very bad: I hope all is not true that is charged upon him. Of his behaviour in prison an account will be published. . . .

Yours affectionately,
Sam. Johnson

July 1777-1781

\

The Lives *progressed slowly through 1777 and 1778. They were growing out of all proportion to the projected "little Prefaces," and Johnson cancelled what had by now become his ritual visit to the country in 1778 to stay in town and write. He was not alone: to Levett and Frank and the dying Miss Williams were now added three more charity lodgers. Writing in this peaceless setting, Johnson managed, by March of 1779, to produce the first twenty-two of his fifty-six lives.*

He left for Lichfield in June, blessed with good health for the first time in twenty years; but he was back in town at work by September, "so far as his indolence allowed him to labour." Again, in 1780, he worked on through the summer. "I have sate at home in Bolt-court, all the summer, thinking to write the Lives, and a great

part of the time only thinking." Diversions were legion—his let-
ters bear witness to one of Johnson's healthiest, happiest, and most
active social seasons—but in March 1781 the last six volumes were
done.

It was only days later that Henry Thrale died of an apoplectic
fit. His first seizure had taken place two years before, after which
his wife had hurried him back and forth between Brighton and
Bath. But he would do nothing to preserve his life, a life he had
ceased to enjoy. Johnson begged him to save himself; he fought
Thrale's losing campaign for parliament, he stood at his beside on the
day of his death; later, as his executor, he helped to sell the great
brewery. Garrick, Beauclerk, many friends had died during these
years: but no one who had mattered as much as Thrale.

External events intrude in this period more than commonly. Eng-
land was shamed and impoverished by the American war, and threat-
ened in 1779 with a French invasion. "I have no delight in talking of
publick affairs," he told Boswell in October 1779, and he was not
alone; more than one Briton was convinced that he was living on a
shrinking, sinking island in the late '70s and '80s. In June of 1780
Johnson's letters record the most frightening domestic crisis of the
half-century, the Gordon Riots. London was held, if only for a
few days, under the anarchic spell of the Mob, in a sort of dis-
mal preview of the Paris of '89. In convulsive fits, the eighteenth
century was dying, and Johnson was dying with it.

156. To William Sharp

July 7, 1777

Sir

To the Collection of *English Poets* I have recommended the
volume of Dr. Watts to be added. His name has been long held by
me in *veneration;* and I would not willingly be reduced to tell of
him, only that he was born and died. Yet, of his life I know very
little; and therefore must pass him in a manner very unworthy of
his character, unless some of his friends will favour me with the
necessary information. Many of them must be known to you; and
by your influence perhaps I may obtain some instruction. My plan

does not exact much; but I wish to distinguish *Watts;* a man who never wrote but for a good purpose. Be pleased to do for me what you can.

I am, Sir, your humble servant,
Sam. Johnson.

157. *To Richard Farmer, Cambridge*

July 22, 1777

Sir

The Booksellers of London have undertaken a kind of Body of English Poetry, excluding generally the dramas, and I have undertaken to put before each authour's works a sketch of his life, and a character of his writings. Of some, however I know very little, and am afraid I shall not easily supply my deficiencies. Be pleased to inform me whether among Mr. Bakers manuscripts,[1] or anywhere else at Cambridge any materials are to be found. If any such collection can be gleaned, I doubt not of your willingness to direct our search, and will tell the booksellers to employ a transcriber. If you think my inspection necessary, I will come down, for who that has once experienced the civilities of Cambridge would not snatch the opportunity of another visit?

I am, Sir,
Your most humble servant,
Sam: Johnson

158. *To Joseph Nollekens*

Lichfield, August 29, 1777

Sir

I have at last sent you what remains, to put to poor dear Goldsmiths monument, and hope to see it erected in the abbey.

You promised me a cast of the head.[2] If it could be sent to Lich-

[1] Forty-two folio volumes of manuscript relating to Cambridge men and events, collected by Thomas Baker (1656-1740).

[2] Nollekens' famous bust of Johnson was completed in 1777 and exhibited at the Royal Academy exhibition.

field directed to Mrs Lucy Porter before I leave the country I
should be glad, though the matter is not of such Consequence, as
that you should incommode yourself about it.

I hope Mrs Nollikens and our Friends in Italy are all well, and
that we shall all have some time or other a joyful Meeting.

I am, Sir,

Your most humble Servant

Sam: Johnson

Natus Hibernia, Forneiae Longfordiensis, in loco cui nomen
Pallas, Nov. XXIX, MDCCXXXI.

Eblanae literis institutus,

Obiit Londini, Apr. IV. MDCCLXXIV.[3]

159. To Mrs. Thrale

Ashbourne, September 13, 1777

Dear Madam, . . .

Boswell, I believe, is coming. He talks of being here to-day. I
shall be glad to see him. But he shrinks from the Baltick expedition,[4] which I think is the best scheme in our power. What we
shall substitute, I know not. He wants to see Wales, but except
the woods of Bachycraigh[5] what is there in Wales? What that can
fill the hunger of ignorance, or quench the thirst of curiosity? We
may perhaps form some scheme or other, but, in the phrase of
Hockley in the Hole,[6] it is a pity he has not a better bottom.

Tell my young mistress that this day's letter is too short, and it
brings me no news either foreign or domestick.

[3] "Born in Pallas, Longford County, Ireland, November 29, 1731. Edu-
cated in Dublin, he died in London, April 4, 1774." These are only the
last six lines of Johnson's inscription for Goldsmith. The birthdate is in-
correct.

[4] Boswell had first made the suggestion of a journey to Sweden, Russia,
and the northern regions during their Scottish trip, but now wrote, "I
shrink a little from our scheme of going up the Baltick."

[5] Mrs. Thrale's estate in north Wales.

[6] A bear-baiting and prize-fighting arena in London.

156

I am going to dine with Mr. Dyot, and Frank tells sternly, that it is past two o'clock.

I am, dearest Madam,
Your, &c.

160. To Mrs. Thrale, Brighthelmston

Ashbourne, October 13, 1777

Dear Madam . . .

I cannot but think on your kindness and my Masters. Life has upon the whole fallen short, very short, of my early expectation, but the acquisition of such a Friendship, at an age when new Friendships are seldom acquired, is something better than the general course of things gives Man a right to expect. I think on it with great delight, I am not very apt to be delighted.

I am, Madam
Your most obedient Servant
Sam: Johnson

161. To Mrs. Thrale, Brighthelmston

Lichfield, October 27, 1777

Dear Madam

You talk of writing and writing as if you had all the writing to yourself. If our Correspondence were printed I am sure Posterity, for Posterity is always the authours favourite, would say that I am a good writer too. Anch' io sonô Pittore.[7] To sit down so often with nothing to say, to say something so often, almost without consciousness of saying, and without any remembrance of having said, is a power of which I will not violate my modesty by boasting, but I do not believe that every body has it.

Some when they write to their friends are all affection, some are wise and sententious, some strain their powers for efforts of gayety, some write news, and some write secrets, but to make a letter with-

[7] "I *too* am a painter!" Attributed to Correggio, on first seeing Raphael's "Saint Cecilia" in Bologna.

out affection, without wisdom, without gayety, without news, and without a secret is, doubtless, the great epistolick art. . . .

162. To William Strahan

July 27, 1778

Sir,

It would be very foolish for us to continue strangers any longer. You can never by persistency make wrong right. If I resented too acrimoniously, I resented only to yourself. Nobody ever saw or heard what I wrote. You saw that my anger was over, for in a day or two I came to your house. I have given you longer time; and I hope you have made so good use of it, as to be no longer on evil terms with,

Sir, Your, &c.
Sam. Johnson.[8]

163. To James Elphinston

July 27, 1778

Sir

Having myself suffered what you are now suffering, I well know the weight of your distress, how much need you have of comfort, and how little comfort can be given.[9] A loss, such as yours, lacerates the mind, and breaks the whole system of purposes and hopes. It leaves a dismal vacuity in life, which affords nothing on which the affections can fix, or to which endeavour may be directed. All this I have known, and it is now, in the vicissitude of things, your turn to know it.

But in the condition of mortal beings, one must lose another. What would be the wretchedness of life, if there was not something always in view, some Being, immutable and unfailing, to whose mercy man may have recourse. Τὸν πρῶτον κινοῦντα ἀκίνητον.[10]

[8] The circumstances of the quarrel are unknown.
[9] Elphinston's wife had just died.
[10] "The prime mover is himself unmoved." (Aristotle.)

Here we must rest. The greatest Being is the most benevolent. We must not grieve for the dead as men without hope, because we know that they are in his hands. We have, indeed, not leisure to grieve long, because we are hastening to follow them. Your race and mine have been interrupted by many obstacles, but we must humbly hope for an happy end.

I am, Sir,

Your most humble servant,

Sam: Johnson.

164. To John Nichols

July 27, 1778

Sir

You have now all *Cowley.* I have been drawn to a great length, but Cowley or Waller never had any critical examination before. I am very far advanced in *Dryden,* who will be long too. The next great life I purpose to be *Milton's.*

It will be kind if you will gather the Lives of *Denham, Butler,* and *Waller,* and bind them in half binding in a small volume, and let me have it to shew my friends, as soon as may be. I sincerely hope the press shall stand no more.

I am, Sir,

Your most humble servant,

Sam: Johnson.

165. To Mrs. Thrale, Brighthelmston

November 14, 1778

Dearest Madam

. . . We have tolerable concord at home, but no love. Williams hates every body. Levet hates Desmoulins and does not love Williams. Desmoulins hates them both. Poll[11] loves none of them. . . .

[11] Carmichael.

166. To John Nichols

November 23, 1778

Mr Johnson will hope for Mr Nichols' company to tea, about six this afternoon, to talk of the Index, and settle the terms.

167. To Eva Maria Garrick

February 2, 1779

Dr Johnson sends most respectful condolence to Mrs Garrick, and wishes that any endeavour of his could enable her support a loss which the world cannot repair.[12]

168. To Mrs. Thrale

March 10, 1779

. . . I got my lives, not yet quite printed, put neatly together, and sent them to the King, what he says of them I know not. Mr Barnard could not speak to him. If the King is a Whig, he will not like them; but is any King a Whig? . . .

169. To John Wesley, Edinburgh

May 3, 1779

Sir

Mr. Boswell, a gentleman who has been long known to me, is desirous of being known to you, and has asked this recommendation, which I give him with great willingness, because I think it very much to be wished that worthy and religious men should be acquainted with each other.

I am, Sir,
Your most humble servant,
Sam. Johnson.

[12] David Garrick died January 20, 1779. His was a death, Johnson wrote, "which has eclipsed the gaiety of nations, and impoverished the publick stock of harmless pleasure."

170. To Lucy Porter, Lichfield

August 24, 1779

Dear Madam

I suppose you are all frighted at Lichfield and indeed the terrour has been very general, but I am still of opinion that there is not yet any danger of invasion. The French fleet were within sight of Plymouth, but no gun was, I believe fired on either side. I had a note from Mr Chamier (the under Secretary of State) yesterday, that tells me. *The combined fleets* (of French and Spaniards) *are not in sight of land. They are supposed to be driven out of the channel by the Easterly wind.*

The English fleet under Hardy is much inferiour to that of the Enemy in number of vessels, but our Ships are said to have greater guns, and to be better manned. The Battle, whenever it happens, will be probably of greater consequence than any battle in our time. If the French get the better we shall perhaps be invaded, and must fight for ourselves upon our own ground, if Hardy prevails all danger of that kind is at an end. If we are invaded the King is said to have resolved that he will head his own army.

Do not pay any regard to the newspapers; you will only disturb yourself. When there is any thing worth telling you, I design to let you know it. At present, it is the general opinion that the first action of consequence will be a great naval battle, and till that is over, all other designs, whatever they are, will be suspended.[13]

I am, Dear Madam, your humble Servant

Sam: Johnson.

[13] The combined French and Spanish fleets of some 60 or 70 ships lay off Plymouth from June through August of this year. Although they easily outnumbered the English Channel Fleet, and had little to fear from the Plymouth garrison, they never attempted the anticipated invasion. The fear of it, however, was enough to paralyze the government.

171. To Mrs. Thrale, Brighthelmston

November 8, 1779

Dear Madam . . .

Of the capture of Jamaica nothing is known, nor do I think it probable or possible.[14] How the French should in a few days take from us an Island, which We could not in almost a century take from a few fugitive Negroes whom the Spaniards left behind them, is not easily imagined. If you stay much longer in Sussex you may perhaps hear that London is taken. . . .

172. To Mrs. Thrale, Bath

April 6, 1780

Dearest Lady . . .

I have not quite neglected my Lives. Addison is a long one but it is done. Prior is not short, and that is done too. I am upon Rowe, who cannot fill much paper. If I have done them before you come again, I think to bolt upon you at Bath, for I shall not be now afraid of Mrs. Cotton. Let Burney take care that she does me no harm. . . .

173. To James Boswell, Edinburgh

April 8, 1780

Dear Sir

Well, I had resolved to send you the Chesterfield letter; but I will write once again without it. Never impose tasks upon mortals. To require two things is the way to have them both undone. . . .

Poor dear Beauclerk—*nec, ut soles, dabis joca.*[15] His wit and his folly, his acuteness and maliciousness, his merriment and reasoning, are now over. Such another will not often be found among mankind. He directed himself to be buried by the side of his mother, an instance of tenderness which I hardly expected. He has left his children to the care of Lady Di. and if she dies, of Mr. Langton, and

---

[14] The island was not in fact taken, despite rumors to the contrary.

[15] "You will jest no more, as you used to do." (From the Dying Hadrian's Address to his Soul.)

of Mr. Leicester, his relation, and a man of good character. His library has been offered to sale to the Russian ambassador.

Dr. Percy, notwithstanding all the noise of the newspapers, has had no literary loss. Clothes and moveables were burnt to the value of about one hundred pounds; but his papers, and I think his books, were all preserved.

Poor Mr. Thrale has been in extreme danger from an apoplectical disorder, and recovered, beyond the expectation of his physicians; he is now at Bath, that his mind may be quiet, and Mrs. Thrale and Miss are with him.

Having told you what has happened to your friends, let me say something to you of yourself. You are always complaining of melancholy, and I conclude from those complaints that you are fond of it. No man talks of that which he is desirous to conceal, and every man desires to conceal that of which he is ashamed. Do not pretend to deny it; *manifestum habemus furem;*[16] make it an invariable and obligatory law to yourself, never to mention your own mental diseases; If you are never to speak of them you will think on them but little, and if you think little of them, they will molest you rarely. When you talk of them, it is plain that you want either praise or pity; for praise there is no room, and pity will do you no good; therefore, from this hour speak no more, think no more about them. . . .

174. *To Mrs. Thrale, Bath*

April 11, 1780

Dear Madam

On Sunday I dined with poor Lawrence who is deafer than ever. When he was told that Dr Moisy visited Mr Thale he enquired, for what? and said that there was nothing to be done, which Nature would not do for herself. On Sunday evening I was at Mrs Vesey's and there was enquiry about my Master, but I told them all good. There was Dr. Barnard of Eaton, and we made a noise all the evening, and there was Pepys, and Wraxal till I drove him away. And I

---

[16] "We have the manifest thief," i.e., the thief has confessed. A legal phrase.

have no loss of my mistress, who laughs, and frisks, and frolicks it all the long day, and never thinks of poor Colin.[17]

If Mr Thrale will but continue to mend we shall, I hope, come together again, and do as good things as ever we did, but perhaps you will be made too proud to heed me, and yet, as I have often told you, it will not be easy for you to find such another.

Queeney has been a good Girl, and wrote me a letter; if Burney said she would write, she told you a fib. She writes nothing to me. She can write home fast enough. I have a good mind not to let her know, that Dr Bernard,[18] to whom I had recommended her novel, speaks of it with great commendation, and that the copy which she lent me, has been read by Dr Lawrence three times over. And yet what a Gypsey it is. She no more minds me than if I were a Brangton.[19] Pray speak to Queeney to write again.

I have had a cold and a cough, and taken opium, and think I am better. We have had very cold weather, bad riding weather for my Master, but he will surmount it all. Did Mrs Browne make any reply to your comparison of business with solitude, or did you quite down her? I am much pleased to think that Mrs. Cotton thinks me worth a frame, and a place upon her wall. Her kindness was hardly within my hope, but time does wonderful things. All my fear is, that if I should come again, my print would be taken down. I fear, I shall never hold it.

Who dines with you? Do you see Dr. Woodward or Dr. Harrington? Do you go to the House where they write for the myrtle?[20] You are at all places of high resort, and bring home hearts by

[17] A reference to the pastoral hero of Nicholas Rowe's poem, "Colin's Complaint":

> Then to her new love let her go;
> And deck her in golden array;
> Be finest at every fine show
> And frolic it all the long day.

[18] Edward Barnard. Fanny Burney's first novel *Evelina* was the hit of the season.

[19] The Branghtons are a family of vilely-mannered, middle-class boors in *Evelina*.

[20] Fashionable guests at Sir John and Lady Miller's villa, Batheaston, wrote poems in competition for myrtle wreaths.

dozens; while I am seeking for something to say about men of whom I know nothing but their verses, and sometimes very little of them. Now I have begun however, I do not despair of making an end. Mr. Nichols holds that Addison is the most *taking* of all that I have done. I doubt they will not be done before you come away.

Now you think yourself the first Writer in the world for a letter about nothing. Can you write such a letter as this? So miscellaneous, with such noble disdain of regularity, like Shakespeare's works, such graceful negligence of transition like the ancient enthusiasts. The pure voice of nature and of friendship. Now of whom shall I proceed to speak? Of whom but Mrs. Montague, having mentioned Shakespeare and Nature does not the name of Montague force itself upon me? Such were the transitions of the ancients, which now seem abrupt because the intermediate idea is lost to modern understandings. I wish her name had connected itself with friendship, but, ah Colin thy hopes are in vain, one thing however is left me, I have skill to complain,[21] but I hope I shall not complain much while you have any kindness for me.

I am,

Dearest and dearest Madam

Your most humble servant

Sam: Johnson.

You do not date your letters.

175. To Mrs. Thrale, Bath

April 25, 1780

Dear Madam . . .

How do you think I live? On Thursday I dined with Hamilton, and went thence to Mrs. Ord. On Friday, with much company at Reynolds's. On Saturday, at Dr. Bell's. On Sunday, at Dr. Burney's, with your two sweets from Kensington,[22] who are both well; at

[21] From Rowe's "Colin's Complaint":

> What though I have skill to complain . . .
> Ah, Colin! Thy hopes are in vain . . .

[22] Two of Mrs. Thrale's young daughters were at school in Kensington.

night came Mrs. Ord, Mr. Harris, and Mr. Greville, &c. On Monday, with Reynolds, at night with Lady Lucan; to-day with Mr. Langton; to-morrow with the Bishop of St. Asaph; on Thursday with Mr. Bowles; Friday, ———; Saturday, at the Academy; Sunday, with Mr. Ramsay.

I told Lady Lucan how long it was since she sent to me; but she said I must consider how the world rolls about her. She seemed pleased that we met again. . . .

I not only scour the town from day to day, but many visitors come to me in the morning; so that my work makes no great progress, but I will try to quicken it. I should certainly like to bustle a little among you, but I am unwilling to quit my post till I have made an end.

You did not tell me in your last letter how Mr. Thrale goes on. If he will be *ruled, for aught appears, he may live on these hundred years.*[23] Fix him when he comes in alternate diet.

I am, dearest Lady, Your, &c.

London, April 25, 1780.

Now there is a date; look at it.

176. To Mrs. Thrale, Bath

May 1, 1780

Dearest Madam . . .

At Mrs. Ord's I met one Mrs. Buller, a travelled lady, of great spirit, and some consciousness of her own abilities. We had a contest of gallantry an hour long, so much to the diversion of the company, that at Ramsay's last night, in a crowded room, they would have pitted us again. There were Smelt, and the Bishop of St. Asaph, who comes to every place; and Lord Monboddo, and Sir Joshua, and ladies out of tale.

The exhibition, how will you do, either to see or not to see! The exhibition is eminently splendid. There is contour, and keeping, and grace, and expression, and all the varieties of artificial excellence. The appartments were truly very noble. The pictures, for

---

[23] Paraphrased from Swift's "Verses on the Death of Dr. Swift."

the sake of a sky light, are at the top of the house; there we dined, and I sat over against the Archbishop of York. See how I live when I am not under petticoat government.

I am, &c.

London, May 1, 1780.
Mark that—you did not put the year to your last.

177. *To Mrs. Thrale, Bath*

May 9, 1780

Dear Madam . . .

My Lives creep on. I have done Addison, Prior, Rowe, Granville, Sheffield, Collins, Pit, and almost Fenton. I design to take Congreve now into my hand. I hope to have done before you come home, and then whither shall I go? . . .

178. *To John Nichols*

(May 1780?)

Sir

In reading Rowe in your Edition, which is very impudently called mine, I observed a little piece unnaturally and odiously obscene.[25] I was offended, but was still more offended when I could

[25] Johnson had little voice in the selection of poets or poems, and thus resented the edition's being advertised as "Johnson's Poets." The "little piece" is an "Epigram on a Lady who shed her Water at seeing the Tragedy of CATO":

> Whilst maudlin Whigs deplore their CATO's Fate,
> Still with dry Eyes the Tory CELIA sate:
> But tho' her Pride forbad her Eyes to flow,
> The gushing Waters found a Vent below.
> Tho' secret yet with copious Streams she mourns,
> Like twenty River-Gods with all their Urns.
> Let others screw an hypocritic Face,
> She shews her grief in a sincerer Place!
> Here Nature reigns, and Passion void of Art;
> For this Road leads directly to the Heart.

Johnson was mistaken: the poem was by Rowe.

not find it in Rowe's genuine volumes. To admit it had been wrong, to interpolate it is surely worse. If I had known of such a piece in the whole collection I should have been angry. What can be done?

179. *To Mrs. Thrale, Bath*

May 25, 1780

Dear Madam . . .

A Lady has sent me a vial like Mrs Nesbit's vial, of essence of roses. What am I come to?

Congreve, whom I dispatched at the Borough, while I was attending the election, is one of the best of the little lives; but then I had your conversation.

You seem to suspect that I think You too earnest about the success of your solicitation: if I gave you any reason for that suspicion it was without intention. It would be with great discontent that I should see Mr Thrale decline the representation of the borough, and with much greater should I see him ejected. To sit in Parliament for Southwark is the highest honour that his station permits him to attain, and his ambition to attain it is surely rational and laudable. I will not say that for an honest man to struggle for a vote in the legislature, at a time when honest votes are so much wanted, is absolutely a duty, but it is surely an act of virtue. The Expence, if it were more, I should wish him to despise. Money is made for such purposes as this. and the method to which the trade is now brought, will, I hope, secure him from any want of what he shall now spend.

Keep Mr. Thrale well, and make him keep himself well, and put all other care out of your dear head. . . .

180. To Mrs. Thrale, Bath

June 9, 1780

Dear Madam

To the question who was impressed with consternation it may with great truth be answered that every body was impressed, for nobody was sure of his safety.[26]

On Friday the good Protestants met in St George's Fields at the summons of Lord George Gordon, and marching to Westminster insulted the Lords and Commons, who all bore it with great tameness. At night the outrages began by the demolition of the mass-house[27] by Lincolns Inn.

An exact Journal of a week's defiance of Government I cannot give you. On Monday Mr Strahan who had been insulted spoke to Lord Mansfield, who had I think been insulted too, of the licentiousness of the populace, and his Lordship treated it as a very slight irregularity. On Tuesday night they pulled down Fielding's house and burnt his goods in the Street. They had gutted on Monday Sir George Savile's house but the building was saved. On Tuesday evening, leaving Fielding's ruins they went to Newgate to demand their companions who had been seized demolishing the Chapel. The Keeper could not release them but by the Mayor's permission which he went to ask, at his return he found all the prisoners released, and Newgate in a blaze. They then went to Bloomsbury and

---

[26] Lord George Gordon, a twenty-nine-year-old Scotch Presbyterian fanatic obsessed by the chimera of Catholic subversion, led a London mob to Parliament on June 2 to present a petition of protest against George Savile's Roman Catholic Relief Act. He managed to incite his mob first to insults, then to violence: it soon grew out of all control. While the army and the civic magistrates argued back and forth over whose problem it was, the riots proceeded unstemmed in very much the manner described in Johnson's letters. The King in council broke the deadlock on June 7 by ordering out the troops, with or without civic concurrence; he merits Johnson's praise (as, apparently, does John Wilkes). The mob was finally beaten on June 9, after a week of civic anarchy, and London was brought reasonably back to normal by June 12. Four hundred fifty-eight people were killed or wounded, and fifty-nine rioters were sentenced to death.

[27] Catholic chapel.

fastened upon Lord Mansfield's house, which they pulled down and as for his goods they totally burnt them. They have since gone to Cane Wood,[28] but a guard was there before them. They plundered some papists I think, and burnt a Masshouse in Moorfields the same night.

On Wednesday I walked with Dr Scot to look at Newgate, and found it in ruins, with the fire yet glowing. As I went by, the protestants were plundering the Sessionshouse at the old Bailey. There were not I believe a hundred, but they did their work at leisure, in full security, without sentinels, without trepidation, as Men lawfully employed, in full day. Such is the Cowardice of a commercial place. On Wednesday they broke open the Fleet and the King's bench and the Marshalsea, and Woodstreet counter and Clerkenwell Bridewell,[29] and released all the prisonners.

At night they set fire to the Fleet, and to the King's bench, and I know not how many other places; You might see the glare of conflagration fill the sky from many parts. The Sight was dreadful. Some people were threatned, Mr. Strahan moved what he could, and advised me to take care of myself. Such a time of terrour You have been happy in not seeing.

The King said in Council that the Magistrates had not done their duty, but that he would do his own, and a proclamation was published directing us to keep our Servants within doors, as the peace was now to be preserved by force. The Soldiers were sent out to different parts, and the town is now at quiet.

What has happened at your house you will know, the harm is only a few buts of beer, and I think, you may be sure that the danger is over. There is a body of Soldiers at St Margaret's hill. . . .

[28] Lord Mansfield's suburban estate.
[29] These are all London prisons.

181. To Mrs. Thrale, Bath

June 10, 1780

Dear Madam

You have ere now heard and read enough to convince you, that we have had something to suffer, and something to fear, and therefore I think it necessary to quiet the solicitude which you undoubtedly feel, by telling that our calamities and terrors are now at an end. The Soldiers are stationed so as to be every where within call; there is no longer any body of rioters, and the individuals are hunted to their holes, and led to prison; the streets are safe and quiet; Lord George was last night sent to the Tower. Mr. John Wilkes was this day with a party of soldiers in my neighbourhood, to seize the publisher of a seditious paper. Every body walks, and eats, and sleeps in security. But the history of last week would fill you with amazement, it is without any modern example.

Several Chapels have been destroyed, and several inoffensive papists have been plundered, but the high sport was to burn the Jayls. This was a good rabble trick. The Debtors and the Criminals were all set at liberty, but of the Criminals, as has always happened, many are already retaken, and two Pirates have surrendered themselves, and it is expected that they will be pardoned.

Government now acts again with its proper force; and we are all again under the protection of the King and the Laws. I thought that it would be agreeable to you and my master to have my testimony to the publick security; and that you would sleep more quietly when I told you that you are safe.

I am, dearest Lady, Your, &c.

182. To Mrs. Thrale, Brighthelmston

June 12, 1780

Dear Madam

All is well, and all is likely to continue well. The streets are all quiet, and the houses are all safe. This is a true answer to the first enquiry which obtrudes itself upon your tongue at the reception of a letter from London. The publick has escaped a very heavy calamity. The rioters attempted the Bank on Wednesday night, but in no great number; and like other thieves, with no great resolution. Jack Wilkes headed the party that drove them away. It is agreed, that if they had seized the Bank on Tuesday, at the height of the panick, when no resistance had been prepared, they might have carried irrecoverably away whatever they had found. Jack, who was always zealous for order and decency, declares, that if he be trusted with power, he will not leave a rioter alive. There is however now no longer any need of heroism or bloodshed; no blue riband is any longer worn.[30]

[Lady Lade] called on Friday at Mrs. Gardiner's, to see how she escaped or what she suffered; and told her, that she had herself too much affliction within doors, to take much notice of the disturbances without.

It was surely very happy that you and Mr. Thrale were away in the tumult; you could have done nothing better than has been done, and must have felt much terrour which your absence has spared you.

We have accounts here of great violences committed by the Protestants at Bath; and of the demolition of the masshouse. We have seen so much here, that we are very credulous.

Pray tell Miss Burney that Mr. Hutton called on me yesterday, and spoke of her with praise; not profuse, but very sincere, just as I do. And tell Queeney, that if she does not write oftener, I will try to forget her. There are other pretty girls that perhaps I could get, if I were not constant.

My Lives go on but slowly. I hope to add some to them this week. I wish they were well done.

Thus far I had written when I received your letter of battle and conflagration. You certainly do right in retiring; for who can guess the caprice of the rabble? My master and Queeney are dear people for not being frighted, and you and Burney are dear people for being frighted. I wrote to you a letter of intelligence and consolation; which, if you staid for it, you had on Saturday; and

[30] The rioter's identifying armband or cockade; non-demonstrators wore it for protection against the mob. ("I am decking myself with blue ribbons like a May-day garland," wrote Walpole.)

I wrote another on Saturday, which perhaps may follow you from Bath, with some atchievement of John Wilkes.

Do not be disturbed; all danger here is apparently over: but a little agitation still continues. We frighten one another with seventy thousand Scots to come hither with the Dukes of Gordon and Argyle, and eat us, and hang us, or drown us; but we are all at quiet. . . .

Of the commotions at Bath there has been talk here all day. An express must have been sent; for the report arrived many hours before the post, at least before the distribution of the letters. This report I mentioned in the first part of my letter, while I was yet uncertain of the fact.

When it is known that the rioters are quelled in London, their spirit will sink in every other place, and little more mischief will be done.

I am, dear Madam, Your, &c.

183. *To Mrs. Thrale, Brighthelmston*

June 14, 1780

Dear Madam

Every thing here is safe and quiet. This is the first thing to be told; and this I told in my last letter directed to Brighthelmstone. There has indeed been an universal panick, from which the King was the first that recovered. Without the concurrence of his ministers, or the assistance of the civil magistrate, he put the soldiers in motion, and saved the town from calamities, such as a rabble's government must naturally produce.

Now you are at ease about the publick, I may tell you that I am not well; I have had a cold and cough some time, but it is grown so bad, that yesterday I fasted and was blooded, and to day took physick and dined: but neither fasting nor bleeding, nor dinner, nor physick, have yet made me well.

No sooner was the danger over, than the people of the Borough found out how foolish it was to be afraid, and formed themselves into four bodies for the defence of the place; through which they now march morning and evening in a martial manner.

I am glad to find that Mr. Thrale continues to grow better; if he is well, I hope we shall be all well: but I am weary of my cough, though I have had much worse.

I am, &c.

184. To Mrs. Thrale, Brighthelmston

July 27, 1780

. . . I dined yesterday at Sir Joshua's with Mrs Cholmondely, and she told me, I was the best critick in the world, and I told her, that nobody in the world could judge like her of the merit of a Critick. . . .

185. To Mrs. Thrale, Brighthelmston

August 1, 1780

Madam . . .

Now August and autumn are begun, and the Virgin takes possession of the sky. Will the Virgin do any thing for a man of seventy? I have a great mind to end my work under the Virgin. . . .

186. To Mrs. Thrale, Brighthelmston

August 14, 1780

Dear Madam . . .

I hope you have no design of stealing away to Italy before the election nor of leaving me behind you, though I am not only seventy, but seventy-one. Could not you let me lose a year in round numbers. Sweetly, sweetly, sings Dr Swift

> Some dire misfortune to portend,
> No enemy can match a friend.[31]

But what if I am seventy two, I remember Sulpitius says of Saint Martin (now that's above your reading) est animus victor

[31] "Verses on the Death of Dr. Swift." The verse reads "Some great misfortune."

annorum, et senectuti cedere nescius.[32] Match me that among your young folks. If you try to plague me I shall tell you that according to Galen life begins to decline from *thirty five.* . . .

187. *To James Boswell, Edinburgh*

August 21, 1780

Dear Sir,

I find you have taken one of your fits of taciturnity, and have resolved not to write till you are written to; it is but a peevish humour, but you shall have your way.

I have sate at home in Bolt-court, all the summer, thinking to write the Lives, and a great part of the time only thinking. Several of them, however, are done, and I still think to do the rest.

Mr. Thrale and his family have, since his illness, passed their time first at Bath, and then at Brighthelmston; but I have been at neither place. I would have gone to Lichfield, if I could have had time, and I might have had time, if I had been active; but I have missed much, and done little.

In the late disturbances, Mr. Thrale's house and stock were in great danger; the mob was pacified at their first invasion, with about fifty pounds in drink and meat; and at their second, were driven away by the soldiers. Mr. Strahan got a garrison into his house, and maintained them a fortnight; he was so frighted that he removed part of his goods. Mrs. Williams took shelter in the country.

I know not whether I shall get a ramble this autumn; it is now about the time when we were travelling. I have, however, better health than I had then, and hope you and I may yet shew ourselves in some part of Europe, Asia, or Africa. In the mean time let us play no trick, but keep each other's kindness by all means in our power.

The bearer of this is Dr. Dunbar, of Aberdeen, who has written and published a very ingenious book, and who I think has a kindness for me, and will when he knows you have a kindness for you.

[32] "Though old men are unable to retire, the soul can still conquer one's years."

I suppose your little ladies are grown tall; and you son is become a learned young man. I love them all, and I love your naughty lady, whom I never shall persuade to love me. When the Lives are done, I shall send them to complete her collection, but must send them in paper, as for want of a pattern, I cannot bind them to fit the rest.

> I am, Sir,
> Your most affectionately
> *Sam. Johnson*

188. To Mrs. Thrale, Brighthelmston

August 24, 1780

Dear Madam . . .

The expedition to foreign parts you will not much encourage, and you need not, I think, make any great effort to oppose it, for it is as likely to put us out of the way to mischief as to bring us into it. We can have no projects in Italy. Exercise may relieve the body, and variety will amuse the mind. The expence will not be greater than at home in the regular course of life. And we shall be safe from Brownes and Guilds,[33] and all instigators to schemes of waste. Si te fata ferant, fer fata—[34]

The chief wish that I form is, that Mr Thrale could be made to understand his real state, to know that he is tottering upon a point, to consider every change of his mental character as the symptom of a disease; to distrust any opinions or purposes that shoot up in his thoughts; to think that violent Mirth is the foam, and deep sadness the subsidence of a morbid fermentation; to watch himself, and counteract by experienced remedies every new tendency, or uncommon sensation. This is a new and an ungrateful employment, but without this self examination he never can be safe. You must try to teach it and he to learn it gradually, and in this my sweet Queeny must help you; I am glad to hear of her vigilance and observation. She is my Pupil. . . .

[33] Probably the names of speculators who preyed upon Thrale.

[34] From a Latin epigram by George Buchanan. "If the Fates compel you, bear your fate."

189. *To William Strahan*

September 13, 1780

Sir,

Having lost our Election at Southwark[35] we are looking for a Borough less uncertain. If you can find by enquiry any seat to be had, as seats are had without natural interest, you will by giving immediate notice do a great favour to Mr. Thrale. The messenger shall call to-morrow for your answer. There are, I suppose, men who transact these affairs, but we do not know them. Be so kind as to give us what information you can.

I am, Sir,

Your humble servant,

Sam: Johnson.

190. *To James Boswell, Edinburgh*

October 17, 1780

Dear Sir

I am sorry to write you a letter that will not please you, and yet it is at last what I resolve to do. This year must pass without an interview; the summer has been foolishly lost, like many other of my summers and winters. I hardly saw a green field, but staid in town to work, without working much.

Mr. Thrale's loss of health has lost him the election; he is now going to Brighthelmston, and expects me to go with him, and how long I shall stay I cannot tell. I do not much like the place, but yet I shall go, and stay while my stay is desired. We must, therefore, content ourselves with knowing what we know as well as man can know the mind of man, that we love one another, and that we wish each other's happiness, and that the lapse of a year cannot lessen our mutual kindness. . . .

[35] Thrale placed third in a contest for two seats, with 769 votes to 1177 for the first-place Sir Richard Hotham, a hatter and India merchant. Thrale's illness and inability to campaign had obviously hurt.

191. To Mary Prowse, Frome

December 9, 1780

Madam

I return you very sincere and respectful thanks for all your favours. You have, I see, sent guineas when I expected only pounds.

It was beside my intention that you should make so much enquiry after Johnson.[36] What can be known of him must start up by accident. He was not a Native of your town or country, but an adventurer who came from a distant part in quest of a livelihood, and did not stay a year. He came in 36. and went away in 37. He was likely enough to attract notice while he staid, as a lively noisy man, that loved company. His memory might probably continue for some time in some favourite alehouse. But after so many years perhaps there is no man left that remembers him. He was my near relation.

The unfortunate woman[37] for whom your excellent Mother has so kindly made provision is, in her way, well. I am now sending her some cloaths. Of her cure there is no hope.

Be pleased, Madam, to accept the good wishes and grateful regard of,

Madam,

Your most obedient and most humble Servant,

Sam: Johnson.

192. To Warren Hastings, India

January 29, 1781

Sir

Amidst the importance and multiplicity of affairs in which your great Office engages you I take the liberty of recalling your attention for a moment to literature, and will not prolong the interruption by an apology which your character makes needless.

Mr. Hoole, a Gentleman long known and long esteemed in the India house, after having translated Tasso, has undertaken Ariosto.

[36] Nathaniel Johnson, his brother.
[37] Elizabeth Herne.

How well he is qualified for his undertaking he has already shown. He is desirous Sir, of your favour in promoting his proposals, and flatters me by supposing that my testimony may advance his interest.

It is a new thing for a Clerk of the India house to translate Poets. It is new for a Governour of Bengal to patronise Learning. That he may find his ingenuity rewarded, and that Learning may flourish under your protection is the wish of,

> Sir,
> Your most humble servant,
> *Sam: Johnson*

193. To William Strahan

> *March 5, 1781*

Sir

Having now done my lives I shall have money to receive, and shall be glad to add to it, what remains due for the Hebrides, which you cannot charge me with grasping very rapaciously. The price was two hundred Guineas or pounds; I think first pounds then Guineas. I have had one hundred.

There is likewise something due for the political pamphlets, which I left without bargain to your liberality and Mr Cadel's. Of this you will likewise think that I may have all together.

> I am, Sir,
> Your humble servant
> *Sam: Johnson*

194. To James Boswell, Edinburgh

> *March 14, 1781*

Dear Sir

I hoped you had got rid of all this hypocrisy of misery. What have you to do with Liberty and Necessity? Or what more than to hold your tongue about it? Do not doubt but I shall be most heartily glad to see you here again, for I love every part about you but your affectation of distress.

I have at last finished my Lives, and have laid up for you a load of copy, all out of order, so that it will amuse you a long time to set it right. Come to me, my dear Bozzy, and let us be as happy as we can. We will go again to the Mitre, and talk old times over.

I am, dear Sir,

Yours, affectionately,

Sam. Johnson.

195. To Sir Joshua Reynolds

April 4, 1781

Mr. Johnson knows that Sir Joshua Reynolds and the other Gentlemen will excuse his incompliance with the Call, when they are told that Mr. Thrale died this morning.

196. To Mrs. Thrale, Brighthelmston

April 5, 1781

Dearest Madam

Of your injunctions to pray for You and write to You I hope to leave neither unobserved, and I hope to find You willing in a short time to alleviate your trouble by some other exercise of the mind. I am not without my part of the calamity. No death since that of my Wife has ever oppressed me like this. But let us remember that we are in the hands of him who knows when to give, and when to take away, who will look upon us with mercy through all our variations of existence, and who invites us to call on him in the day of trouble. Call upon him in this great revolution of life, and call with confidence. You will then find comfort for the past, and support for the future. He that has given You happiness in marriage to a degree of which without personal knowledge, I should have thought the description fabulous, can give You another mode of happiness as a Mother, and at last the happiness of losing all temporal cares in the thoughts of an eternity in heaven.

I do not exhort You to reason yourself into tranquillity, we must first pray, and then labour, first implore the Blessing of God and then employ those means which he puts into our hands. Cultivated ground has few weeds, a mind occupied by lawful business, has little room for useless regret.

We read the will to day, but I will not fill my first letter with any other account than that with all my zeal for your advantage I am satisfied, and that the other executors, more used to consider property than I, commended it for wisdom and equity. Yet why should I not tell You that You have five hundred pounds for your immediate expences, and two thousand pounds a year with both the houses and all the goods?

Let us pray for one another, that the time whether long or short that shall yet be granted us, may be well spent, and that when this life which at the longest is very short, shall come to an end, a better may begin which shall never end.

I am, Dearest Madam,

Your most humble Servant

Sam: Johnson

197. To Mrs. Thrale, Brighthelmston

April 9, 1781

Dearest Madam

That You are gradually recovering your tranquillity is the effect to be humbly expected from trust in God. Do not represent life as darker than it is. Your loss has been very great, but You retain more than almost any other can hope to possess. You are high in the opinion of mankind; You have children from whom much pleasure may be expected, and that you will find many friends You have no reason to doubt. Of my friendship, be it worth more or less, I hope You think yourself certain, without much art or care. It will not be easy for me to repay the benefits that I have received, but I hope to be always ready at your call. Our sorrow has different effects, you are withdrawn into solitude, and I am driven into company. I am afraid of thinking what I have lost. I never had such a friend before. Let me have your prayers and those of my dear Queeny.

The prudence and resolution of your design to return so soon to your business and your duty deserves great praise, I shall communi-

181

cate it on Wednesday to the other Executors. Be pleased to let me know whether you would have me come to Streatham to receive you, or stay here till the next day.

I am Madam,
Your most humble servant,
Sam: Johnson.

198. To Bennet Langton, Rochester

June 16, 1781

Dear Sir

How welcome your account of yourself and your invitation to your new house was to me, I need not tell you, who consider our friendship not only as formed by choice but as matured by time. We have been now long enough acquainted to have many images in common, and therefore to have a source of conversation which neither the learning nor the wit of a new companion can supply.

My Lives are now published, and if you will tell me whither I shall send them that they may come to you, I will take care that You shall not be without them.

You will perhaps be glad to hear, that Mrs. Thrale is disencumbred from her Brewhouse,[38] and that it seemed to the purchaser so far from an evil, that he was content to give for it an hundred and thirty five thousand pounds. Is the Nation ruined?

Please to make my repectful compliments to Lady Rothes, and keep me in the memory of all the little dear family, particularly pretty Mrs Jane.[39]

I am Sir
Your affectionate humble Servant
Sam: Johnson.

[38] It was sold to Messrs. Barclay and Perkins; the firm is now called Courage and Barclay's.
[39] I.e., five-year-old Jenny Langton.

1782-1783

"In 1782, his complaints increased, and the history of his life this year, is little more than a mournful recital of the variations of his illness . . ." "In 1783, he was more severely afflicted than ever." (Boswell.)

Johnson's correspondence grimly records his downhill course through these long two years. Every letter is a sick man's letter: together, their weight is tiresome and morbidly dull. First come ten months of asthmatic attacks, bad nights, painful breathing; then the paralytic stroke in June 1783—"It hath pleased almighty God this morning to deprive me of the powers of speech." Then the grotesque and embarrassing tumor, the terror of the knife, the unexpected relief; and finally, toward the close of 1783, a conjunction of ailments so oppressive as to imprison him in his sickroom for six months to come.

To this we must add the deaths of Levett and Williams, the grow-
ing chill in his relations with Mrs. Thrale, the growing shame of
England; she had signed away America, her ministries were bone-
less and despised, and Johnson was disgusted. There were brief holi-
days at Oxford, Rochester, and Salisbury in these months, a visit
from Boswell in the spring. But the happy years were gone. The
end was obviously near.

199. To Dr. Thomas Lawrence

January 17, 1782

Sir

Our old friend Mr Levett, who was last night eminently cheerful, died this morning. The man who lay in the same room hearing an uncommon noise got up: and tried to make him speak, but without effect, he then called Mr Holder the apothecary, who though, when he came, he thought him dead; opened a vein but could draw no blood. So has ended the long life of a very useful, and very blameless man.

I am Sir
Your most humble servant
Sam: Johnson

200. To Mrs. Margaret Strahan

February 4, 1782

Dear Madam

Mrs Williams showed me your kind letter. This little habitation is now but a melancholy place, clouded with the gloom of disease and death. Of the four inmates one has been suddenly snatched away, two are oppressed by very afflictive and dangerous ilness; and I tried yesterday to gain some relief by a third bleeding from a dis-order which has for some time distressed me, and I think myself today much better. . . .

201. To Edmond Malone

March 2, 1782

Dear Sir

I hope, I grow better, and shall soon be able to enjoy the kindness of my friends. I think this wild adherence to Chatterton[1] more unaccountable than the obstinate defence of Ossian. For Ossian there is a national pride, which may be forgiven though it cannot be applauded: for Chatterton there is nothing but the resolution to say again what has once been said.

I am Sir
Your humble servant
Sam: Johnson

202. To Bennet Langton, Rochester

March 20, 1782

Dear Sir

It is now long since we saw one another, and whatever has been the reason neither You have written to me, nor I to You. To let friendship dye away by negligence and silence is certainly not wise. It is voluntarily to throw away one of the greatest comforts of this weary pilgrimage of which when it is, as it must be taken finally away he that travels on alone will wonder how his esteem could possibly be so little. Do not forget me, You see that I do not forget You. It is pleasing in the silence of solitude to think, that there is One at least however distant of whose benevolence there is little doubt, and whom there is yet hope of seeing again.

Of my Life, from the time when we parted, the history is very mournful. The Spring of last year deprived me of Thrale, a man whose eye for fifteen years had scarcely been turned upon me but with respect or tenderness; for such another friend the general course of human things will not suffer man to hope. I passed the Summer at Streatham but there was no Thrale, and having idled away the summer with a weakly body and neglected mind I made a journey to Staffordshire on the edge of winter. The season was dreary, I was sickly, and found the Friends sickly whom I went to

[1] See Letter 141, n. 7.

see. After a sorrowful sojourn I returned to a habitation possessed for the present by two sick women, where my dear old friend Mr. Levet to whom, as he used to tell me, I owe your acquaintance, died a few weeks ago suddenly in his bed. There passed not, I believe a minute between health and death. At night, as at Mrs. Thrale's I was musing in my chamber, I thought with uncommon earnestness, that however I might alter my mode of life, or whithersoever I might remove, I would endeavour to retain Levet about me, in the morning my servant brought me word that Levet was called to another state, a state for which, I think, he was not unprepared, for he was very useful to the poor. How much soever I valued him, I now wish that I had valued him more.

I have myself been ill more than eight weeks of a disorder from which at the expence of about fifty ounces of blood, I hope, I am now recovering.

You, dear Sir, have I hope a more cheerful scene you see George fond of his book, and the pretty Misses airy and lively, with my own little Jenny equal to the best, and in whatever can contribute to your quiet or pleasure, You have Lady Rothes ready to concur. May whatever You enjoy of good be encreased, and whatever You suffer of evil be diminished.

I am, Dear Sir, your humble Servant
Sam: Johnson

203. To Jane Gastrell and Elizabeth Aston, Lichfield

March 30, 1782

Dearest Ladies . . .

Here are great changes in the great World, but I cannot tell you more than you will find in the papers. The Men are got in, whom I have endeavoured to keep out, but I hope they will do better than their predecessors; it will not be easy to do worse. . . .[2]

---

[2] The ministry of Lord North, often blamed for the loss of America, had fallen after twelve uncertain years, and the more liberal Rockingham Whigs (Burke's party) took over briefly. Johnson loved neither.

204. To Mrs. Thrale

April 24, 1782

Madam

I have been very much out of order since you sent me away; but why should I tell you, who do not care, nor desire to know? I dined with Mr. Paradise on Monday, with the Bishop of St. Asaph yesterday, with the Bishop of Chester I dine to-day, and with the Academy on Saturday, with Mr. Hoole on Monday, and with Mrs. Garrick on Thursday the 2d of May, and then—what care you? *what then?*

The news run, that we have taken seventeen French transports—that Langton's lady is lying down with her eighth child, all alive—and Mrs. Carter's Miss Sharpe is going to marry a schoolmaster sixty-two years old.

Do not let Mr. Piozzi nor any body else put me quite out of your head, and do not think that any body will love you like

Your, &c.

205. To John Taylor, Market Bosworth, Leicestershire

July 8, 1782

Dear Sir

You are doubtless impatient to know the present state of the court. Dr Hunter whom I take to have very good intelligence has just left me, and from him I learn only that all is yet uncertainty and confusion. Fox, you know, has resigned Burke's dismission is expected. I was particularly told that the Cavendishes were expected to be left out in the new settlement.[3] The Doctor spoke, however, with very little confidence, nor do I believe that those who are now busy in the contest can judge of the event. I did not think Rockingham of such importance as that his death should have had such extensive consequences. . . .

[3] Fox, Cavendish, and Burke all resigned on the death of the Marquis of Rockingham, July 1. Taylor had some interest with the great Cavendish family, and had looked to them for preferment.

206. To John Taylor, Market Bosworth

July 22, 1782

Dear Sir . . .

Mr. Burke's family is computed to have lost by this revolution twelve thousand a year. What a rise, and what a fall. Shelburne speaks of him in private with great malignity. . . . Sir Robert Chambers slipped this session through the fingers of revocation, but I am in doubt of his continuance. Shelburne seems to be his enemy. Mrs. Thrale says they will do him no harm. She perhaps thinks there is no harm without hanging. The mere act of recall strips him of eight thousand a year. . . .

207. To John Taylor, Market Bosworth

August 3, 1782

Dear Sir . . .

I have no national news that is not in the papers, and almost all news is bad. Perhaps no nation not absolutely conquered has declined so much in so short a time. We seem to be sinking. Suppose the Irish having already gotten a free trade and an independent parliament,[4] should say we will have a King, and ally ourselves with the house of Bourbon, what could be done to hinder or to overthrow them?

Poor dear Dr Lawrence is gone to die at Canterbury. He has lost his speech, and the action of his right side, with very little hope of recovering them.

We must all go. I was so exhausted by loss of blood, and by successive disorders in the beginning of this year that I am afraid that the remaining part will hardly restore me. I have indeed rather indulged myself too much, and think to begin a stricter regimen. As it is my friends tell me from time to time, that I look better, and

[4] The Irish Parliament was given legislative independence by the Renunciation Act of 1782.

I am very willing to believe them. Do you likewise take care of your health, we cannot well spare one another.

I am, dear Sir,

Yours affectionately,

Sam: Johnson.

208. *To James Boswell, Edinburgh*

September 7, 1782

Dear Sir

I have struggled through this year with so much infirmity of body, and such strong impressions of the fragility of life, that death, wherever it appears, fills me with melancholy; and I cannot hear without emotion, of the removal of any one, whom I have known, into another state.

Your father's death had every circumstance that could enable you to bear it; it was at a mature age, and it was expected; and as his general life had been pious, his thoughts had doubtless for many years past been turned upon eternity. That you did not find him sensible must doubtless grieve you; his disposition towards you was undoubtedly that of a kind, though not of a fond father. Kindness, at least actual, is in our power, but fondness is not; and if by negligence or imprudence you had extinguished his fondness, he could not at will rekindle it. Nothing then remained between you but mutual forgiveness of each other's faults, and mutual desire of each other's happiness. . . .

209. *To John Nichols*

Brighthelmston, October 28, 1782

Dear Sir . . .

What will the Booksellers give me for this new Edition? I know not what to ask.[5] I would have 24 sets bound in plain calf, and figured with number of the volumes. For the rest they may please themselves. . . .

[5] He received an extra hundred pounds for his revisions on the third edition of the *Lives.*

1782-1783

210. *To James Boswell, Edinburgh*

December 7, 1782

Dear Sir

Having passed almost this whole year in a succession of disorders, I went in October to Brighthelmston, whither I came in a state of so much weakness, that I rested four times in walking between the inn and the lodging. By physick and abstinence I grew better, and am now reasonably easy, though at a great distance from health. I am afraid, however, that health begins, after seventy, and often long before, to have a meaning different from that which it had at thirty. But it is culpable to murmur at the established order of the creation, as it is vain to oppose it. He that lives, must grow old; and he that would rather grow old than die, has God to thank for the infirmities of old age. . . .

211. *To Margaret Boswell*

December 7, 1782

Dear Lady

I have not often received so much pleasure as from your invitation to Auchinleck. The journey thither and back is, indeed, too great for the latter part of the year; but if my health were fully recovered, I would suffer no little heat and cold, nor a wet or a rough road to keep me from you. I am, indeed, not without hope of seeing Auchinleck again; but to make it a pleasant place I must see its lady well, and brisk, and airy. For my sake, therefore, among many greater reasons, take care, dear Madam, of your health, spare no expence, and want no attendance that can procure ease, or preserve it. Be very careful to keep your mind quiet; and do not think it too much to give an account of your recovery to

Madam, your, &c.

Sam. Johnson.

212. *To Mrs. Thrale*

December 16, 1782

Madam

My purpose was to have shared the gayety of this evening, and to have heard, Ye Gods! and to have seen, but a very dreadful night has intervened, and as want of sleep has made me very sleepy, it remains for me to dream if I can of Argyle Street.[6]

I am Madam, your most &c
Sam: Johnson

213. *To John Taylor, Ashbourne*

January 21, 1783

Dear Sir

I am glad that your friends are not among the promoters of equal representation, which I consider as specious in theory but dangerous in experiment, as equitable in itself, but above human wisdom to be equitably adjusted, and which is now proposed only to distress the government.[7]

An equal representation can never form a constitution because it can have no stability, for whether you regulate the representation by numbers or by property, that which is equal today, will be unequal in a week.

To change the constituent parts of Government must be always dangerous, for who can tell where changes will stop. A new representation will want the reverence of antiquity, and the firmness of Establishment. The new senate will be considered as Mushrooms which springing in a day may be blasted in a night.

What will a parliament chosen in any new manner, whether more or less numerous, do which is not done by such parliaments as we have? Will it be less tumultuous if we have more, or less mercenary

[6] Mrs. Thrale had leased Streatham, Johnson's haven for so many years, and moved with her daughters to Argyle Street in London.

[7] Pitt's mild proposal for Parliamentary reform was soundly defeated, 293 to 149. "If you do not resist the spirit of innovation in the first attempt, if you admit the smallest and most specious change in our parliamentary system, you are lost." (Edward Gibbon.)

if we have fewer? There is no danger that the parliament as now chosen should betray any of our important rights, and that is all that we can wish.

If the scheme were more reasonable this is not a time for innovation. I am afraid of a civil war. The business of every wise man seems to be now to keep his ground.

I am very glad you are coming.

> I am &c.
> *Sam: Johnson.*

214. *To Sir Joshua Reynolds*

March 4, 1783

Sir

I have sent You back Mr. Crabb's poem[8] which I read with great delight. It is original, vigorous, and elegant.

The alterations which I have made, I do not require him to adopt, for my lines are perhaps not often better than his own, but he may take mine and his own together, and perhaps between them produce something better than either.

He is not to think his copy wantonly defaced. A wet Sponge will wash all the red lines away, and leave the page clear.

His Dedication will be least liked: it were better to contract it into a short sprightly Address.—I do not doubt of Mr. Crabbe's success.

> I am, Sir, your most humble servant,
> *Sam: Johnson.*

215. *To Robert Chambers, Calcutta*

April 19, 1783

Dear Sir

Of the books which I now send you I sent you the first edition, but it fell by the chance of war into the hands of the French. I sent likewise to Mr. Hastings. Be pleased to have these parcels properly delivered.

[8] *The Village.*

Removed as We are with so much land and sea between us, We ought to compensate the difficulty of correspondence by the length of our letters, yet searching my memory, I do not find much to communicate. Of all publick transactions you have more exact accounts than I can give; you know our foreign miscarriages and our intestine discontents, and do not want to be told that we have now neither power nor peace, neither influence in other nations nor quiet amongst ourselves. The state of the Publick, and the operations of government have little influence upon the private happiness of private men, nor can I pretend that much of the national calamities is felt by me; yet I cannot but suffer some pain when I compare the state of this Kingdom, with that in which we triumphed twenty years ago. I have at least endeavoured to preserve order and support Monarchy.

Having been thus allured to the mention of myself, I shall give you a little of my story. That dreadful ilness which seized me at New inn Hall,[9] left consequences which have I think always hung upon me. I have never since cared much to walk. My mental abilities I do not perceive that it impaired. One great abatement of all miseries was the attention of Mr. Thrale, which from our first acquaintance was never intermitted. I passed far the greater part of many years in his house where I had all the pleasure of riches without the solicitude. He took me into France one year, and into Wales another, and if he had lived would have shown me Italy and perhaps many other countries, but he died in the spring of eighty one, and left me to write his epitaph.

But for much of this time my constitutional maladies persued me. My thoughts were disturbed, my nights were insufferably restless, and by spasms in the breast I was condemned to the torture of sleepyness without the power to sleep. These spasms after enduring them more than twenty years I eased by three powerful remedies, abstinence, opium, and mercury, but after a short time they were succeeded by a strange oppression of another kind which when I lay down disturbed me with a sensation like flatulence or intumescence which I cannot describe. To this supervened a difficulty of respira-

[9] In 1770.

tion, such as sometimes makes it painful to cross a street or climb to my chambers; which I have eased by venisection till the Physician forbids me to bleed, as my legs have begun to swel. Almost all the last year past in a succession of diseases 'εκ κακῶν κακά,[10] and this year till within these few days has heaped misery upon me. I have just now a lucid interval.

With these afflictions, I have the common accidents of life to suffer. He that lives long must outlive many, and I am now sometimes to seek for friends of easy conversation and familiar confidence. Mrs. Williams is much worn; Mr. Levet died suddenly in my house about a year ago. Doctor Lawrence is totally disabled by a palsy, and can neither speak nor write. He is removed to Canterbury. Beauclerc died about two years ago and in his last sickness desired to be buried by the side of his Mother. Langton has eight children by Lady Rothes. He lives very little in London, and is by no means at ease. Goldsmith died partly of a fever and partly of anxiety, being immoderately and disgracefully in debt. Dier lost his fortune by dealing in the East India stock, and, I fear, languished into the grave. Boswels father is lately dead, but has left the estate incumbered; Boswel has, I think, five children. He is now paying us his annual visit, he is all that he was, and more. Doctor Scot prospers exceedingly in the commons, but I seldom see him; He is married and has a Daughter.

Jones now Sir William, will give you the present state of the club, which is now very miscellaneous, and very heterogeneous it is therefore without confidence, and without pleasure. I go to it only as to a kind of publick dinner. Reynolds continues to rise in reputation and in riches, but his health has been shaken. Dr. Percy is now Bishop of Dromore, but has I believe lost his only son. Such are the deductions from human happiness.

I have now reached an age which is to expect many diminutions of the good, whatever it be, that life affords; I have lost many friends, I am now either afflicted or threatened by many diseases, but perhaps not with more than are commonly incident to encrease of years, and I am afraid that I bear the weight of time with un-

---

[10] "Evil upon evil."

seemly, if not with sinful impatience. I hope that God will enable me to correct this as well as my other faults, before he calls me to appear before him. . . .

Your old Friend and humble servant,
Sam: Johnson.

216. To Mrs. Thrale, Bath

May 1, 1783

Dear Madam

I am glad that you went to Streatham, though you could not save the dear, pretty, little girl.[11] I loved her, for She was Thrale's and your's, and by her dear Father's appointment in some sort mine; I love you all, and therefore cannot without regret see the phalanx broken, and reflect that You and my other dear Girls are deprived of one that was born your friend. . . .

For some days after your departure I was pretty well, but I have begun to languish again, and last night was very tedious and oppressive. I excused myself today from dining with General Paoli, where I love to dine, but I was griped by the talons of necessity.

On Saturday I dined, as is usual, at the opening of the exhibition. Our company was splendid, whether more numerous than at any former time, I know not. Our Tables seem always full. On monday, if I am told truth, were received at the door one hundred and ninety pounds, for the admission of three thousand eight hundred Spectators. Supposing the show open ten hours, and the Spectators staying one with another each an hour, the rooms never had fewer than three hundred and eighty justling each other. Poor Lowe met some discouragement, but I interposed for him, and prevailed.

Mr Barry's exhibition was opened the same day, and a book is published to recommend it, which, if you read it, you will find

[11] Harriet (Henrietta Sophia) Thrale, age 4, died April 18. Johnson was one of her guardians.

decorated with some satirical pictures of Sir Joshua and others. I have not escaped. You must however think with some esteem of Barry for the comprehension of his design.

I am, Madam,
Your most humble servant
Sam: Johnson

217. *To Edmund Allen*

June 17, 1783

Dear Sir,

It hath pleased almighty God this morning to deprive me of the powers of speech; and, as I do not know but that it may be his farther good pleasure to deprive me soon of my senses, I request you will, on the receipt of this note, come to me, and act for me, as the exigencies of my case may require. I am,

Sincerely Yours,
S. Johnson.

218. *To Mrs. Thrale, Bath*

June 19, 1783

Dear Madam

I am sitting down in no chearful solitude to write a narrative which would once have affected you with tenderness and sorrow, but which you will perhaps pass over now with the careless glance of frigid indifference. For this diminution of regard however, I know not whether I ought to blame You, who may have reasons which I cannot know, and I do not blame myself who have for a great part of human life done You what good I could, and have never done you evil.

I had been disordered in the usual way, and had been relieved by the usual methods, by opium and catharticks, but had rather lessened my dose of opium.

On Monday the 16. I sat for my picture, and walked a considerable way with little inconvenience. In the afternoon and evening I felt myself light and easy, and began to plan schemes of life. Thus

I went to bed, and in a short time waked and sat up as has been long my custom, when I felt a confusion and indistinctness in my head which lasted, I suppose about half a minute; I was alarmed and prayed God, that however he might afflict my body he would spare my understanding. This prayer, that I might try the integrity of my faculties I made in Latin verse. The lines were not very good, but I knew them not to be very good, I made them easily, and concluded myself to be unimpaired in my faculties.

Soon after I perceived that I had suffered a paralytick stroke, and that my Speech was taken from me. I had no pain, and so little dejection in this dreadful state that I wondered at my own apathy, and considered that perhaps death itself when it should come, would excite less horrour than seems now to attend it.

In order to rouse the vocal organs I took two drams. Wine has been celebrated for the production of eloquence; I put myself into violent motion, and, I think, repeated it. But all was vain; I then went to bed, and, strange as it may seem, I think, slept. When I saw light, it was time to contrive what I should do. Though God stopped my speech he left me my hand, I enjoyed a mercy which was not granted to my Dear Friend Laurence, who now perhaps overlooks me as I am writing and rejoices that I have what he wanted. My first note was necessarily to my servant, who came in talking, and could not immediately comprehend why he should read what I put into his hands.

I then wrote a card to Mr Allen, that I might have a discreet friend at hand to act as occasion should require. In penning this note I had some difficulty, my hand, I knew not how nor why, made wrong letters. I then wrote to Dr Taylor to come to me, and bring Dr Heberden, and I sent to Dr Brocklesby, who is my neighbour. My Physicians are very friendly and very disinterested, and give me great hopes, but you may imagine my situation. I have so far recovered my vocal powers, as to repeat the Lord's Prayer with no very imperfect articulation. My memory, I hope, yet remains as it was. But such an attack produces solicitude for the safety of every Faculty.

How this will be received by You I know not, I hope You will sympathise with me, but perhaps

My Mistress gracious, mild, and good,
Cries, Is he dumb? 'tis time he shou'd.[12]

But can this be possible, I hope it cannot. I hope that what, when I could speak, I spoke of You, and to You, will be in a sober and serious hour remembred by You, and surely it cannot be remembred but with some degree of kindness. I have loved you with virtuous affection, I have honoured You with sincere Esteem. Let not all our endearment be forgotten, but let me have in this great distress your pity and your prayers. You see I yet turn to You with my complaints as a settled and unalienable friend, do not, do not drive me from You, for I have not deserved either neglect or hatred.

To the Girls, who do not write often, for Susy has written only once, and Miss Thrale owes me a letter, I earnestly recommend as their Guardian and Friend, that They remember their Creator in the days of their Youth.[13]

I suppose you may wish to know how my disease is treated by the physitians. They put a blister upon my back, and two from my ear to my throat, one on a side. The blister on the back has done little, and those on the throat have not risen. I bullied, and bounced, (it sticks to our last sand) and compelled the apothecary to make his salve according to the Edinburgh dispensatory, that it might adhere better. I have two on now of my own prescription. They likewise give me salt of hartshorn, which I take with no great confidence, but am satisfied that what can be done is done for me.

O God, give me comfort and confidence in Thee, forgive my sins, and if it be thy good pleasure, relieve my diseases for Jesus Christs sake, Amen.

I am almost ashamed of this querulous letter, but now it is written, let it go.

I am, Madam
Your most humble servant
Sam: Johnson.

[12] Paraphrased from Swift's "Verses on the Death of Dr. Swift":

The queen so gracious, mild and good
Cries "is he gone! 'tis time he shou'd."

[13] *Ecclesiastes* 12:1.

219. To James Boswell, Edinburgh

July 3, 1783

Dear Sir Your anxiety about my health is very friendly, and very agreeable with your general kindness. I have, indeed, had a very frightful blow. On the 17th of last month, about three in the morning, as near as I can guess, I perceived myself almost totally deprived of speech. I had no pain. My organs were so obstructed, that I could say *no*, but could scarcely say *yes*. I wrote the necessary directions, for it pleased God to spare my hand, and sent for Dr. Heberden and Dr. Brocklesby. Between the time in which I discovered my own disorder, and that in which I sent for the doctors, I had, I believe, in spite of my surprize and solicitude, a little sleep, and Nature began to renew its operations. They came, and gave the directions which the disease required, and from that time I have been continually improving in articulation. I can now speak, but the nerves are weak, and I cannot continue discourse long; but strength, I hope, will return. The physicians consider me as cured. I was last Sunday at church. On Tuesday I took an airing to Hampstead, and dined with the Club, where Lord Palmerston was proposed, and, against my opinion, was rejected. I design to go next week with Mr. Langton to Rochester, where I purpose to stay about ten days, and then try some other air. I have many kind invitations. Your brother has very frequently enquired after me. Most of my friends have, indeed, been very attentive. Thank dear Lord Hailes for his present.

I hope you found at your return every thing gay and prosperous, and your lady, in particular, quite recovered and confirmed. Pay her my respects.

I am, dear Sir, your most humble servant,

Sam. Johnson.

220. To Mrs. Thrale, Weymouth

August 13, 1783

Dear Madam . . .

I am now broken with disease, without the alleviation of familiar friendship, or domestick society; I have no middle state between clamour and silence, between general conversation and self-torment-ing solitude. Levet is dead, and poor Williams is making haste to dye. I know not if she will ever more come out of her Chamber. I am now quite alone, but let me turn my thoughts another way.

I am, Madam,

Your most humble servant

Sam: Johnson.

221. *To Mrs. Thrale, Weymouth*

August 20, 1783

Madam

This has been a day of great emotion. The office of the Com-munion of the Sick, has been performed in poor Mʳˢ Williams's chamber. She was too weak to rise from her bed, and is therefore to be supposed unlikely to live much longer. She has, I hope, little violent pain, but is wearing out, by torpid inappetence and weari-some decay; but all the powers of her mind are in their full vigour, and when she has spirit enough for conversation, she possesses all the intellectual excellence that she ever had. Surely this is an instance of mercy much to be desired by a parting Soul.

At home I see almost all my companions dead or dying. At Ox-ford I have just lost Wheeler the man with whom I most delighted to converse. The sense of my own diseases, and the sight of the world sinking round me, oppresses me perhaps too much. I hope that all these admonitions will not be vain, and that I shall learn to dye as dear Williams is dying, who was very chearful before and after this aweful solemnity, and seems to resign herself with calmness and hope upon eternal Mercy. . . .

222. *To Mrs. Thrale, Weymouth*

August 26, 1783

Dear Madam

Things stand with me much as they have done for some time. Mrs Williams fancies now and then that she grows better, but her vital powers appear to be slowly burning out. No body thinks, however, that she will very soon be quite wasted, and, as she suffers me to be of very little use to her, I have determined to pass some time with Mr Bowles near Salisbury, and have taken a place for Thursday. Some benefit may be perhaps received from change of air, some from change of company, and some from mere change of place; It is not easy to grow well in a chamber where one has long been sick, and where every thing seen, and every person speaking revives and impresses images of pain. Though it be that no man can run away from himself, he may yet escape from many causes of useless uneasiness. That the *mind is its own place* is the boast of a fallen angel,[14] that had learned to lie. External locality has great effects, at least upon all embodied Beings. I hope this little journey will afford me at least some suspense of melancholy. . . .

223. To John Mudge, Plymouth

Heale, September 9, 1783

Dear Sir

My conviction of your Skill, and my belief of your friendship determine me to intreat your opinion and advice. About the latter end of the year –81, I by some accident perceived that my left testicle was much larger than the right. It for some time encreased slowly but without pain or inconvenience, till at last its bulk made it troublesome. In the beginning of this year it a little incommoded my walk, and considering it as a Hydrocele, I, as soon as more formidable disorders gave me leisure intended to discharge the water; But when I showed it to Cruikshank and Pot, they both suspected, and piercing it at my request with a trocar, they found it to be a sarcocele.[15]

This experiment was made about a month ago, since which time the tumour has encreased both in surface and in weight, and by tension of the skin is extremely tender, and impatient of pressure or friction. Its weight is such as to give great pain, when it is not suspended, and its bulk such as the common dress does but ill conceal,

[14] Milton's Satan, *Paradise Lost.*
[15] Hydrocele, a watery tumor; sarcocele, a malignant growth of tissue.

nor is there any appearance that its growth will stop. It is so hot, that I am afraid it is in a state of perpetual inflammation.

In this state, I with great earnestness desire You to tell me, what is to be done. Excision is doubtless necessary to the case, and I know not any means of palliation. The operation is doubtless painful, but is it dangerous? The pain I hope to endure with decency, but I am loath to put life into much hazard.

Give me, dear Sir, your thoughts upon my case as soon as You can, I shall stay here till I may receive your letter. If You wish to see me, I will come to Plymouth.

My Godson[16] called on me lately. He is weary, and rationally weary of a military life. If You can place him in some other state, I think you may encrease his happiness and secure his virtue. A soldiers time is past in distress and danger, or in idleness and corruption.

I am dear Sir

Your most humble Servant

Sam: Johnson

224. *To Susannah Thrale, Weymouth*

Heale, September 9, 1783

Dear Miss . . .

Pray shew Mamma this passage of a letter from Dr. Brocklesby: "Mrs. Williams, from mere inanition, has at length paid the last debt to Nature, about 3 o'clock this morning (Sept. 6). She died without a struggle, retaining her faculties intire to the very last, and as she expressed it, having set her house in order, was prepared to leave it at the last summons of Nature."

I do not now say any thing more, than that I am,

My Dearest,

Your most humble servant

Sam: Johnson.

---

[16] William Mudge, the doctor's son.

225. *To Bennet Langton, Rochester*

September 24, 1783

Dear Sir

My case, which you guessed at not amiss, is a Sarcocele; a dreadful disorder which however, I hope, God will not suffer to destroy me. Let me have your prayers. I have consulted Mr Mudge of Plymouth who strongly presses an immediate operation. I expect Dr Heberdens advice to morrow. Make my compliments to your dear Lady, to my Jenny, and to all the little ones.

The Gout has within these four days come upon me with a violence, which I never experienced before. It has made me helpless as an infant. It is no great evil in itself but the (——) delays the Chirurgeon.[17]

I am, Sir, Your most &c
Sam: Johnson

226. *To Mrs. Thrale, Bath*

October 9, 1783

Madam

Many reasons hinder me from believing that opium had any part in my late disorder. I had a long time forborn it. I never used it in any quantity comparable to what is taken by those that habitually indulge themselves with it. It never produces palsies by the utmost excess. My Physicians had so little suspicion of it, though they know my practice, that they made use of it to obviate some effects of the blisters.

It was the paralytick affection which I mentioned sixteen year ago to Dr Laurence, when he allowed my fears to be reasonable. It appeared afterward as an asthma, from which since its invasion of another part I have been almost wholly free, and which in its paroxysms was relieved by opium.

The state of the tumour is now changed. When the surgeons visited me, they thought it upon examination a sarcocele, but I was willing to hope something better, and was likewise desirous of

[17] Surgeon.

knowledge rather than conjecture; I therefore proposed an exploration by puncture; the operation was performed, and the unwelcome opinion was confirmed. The breach made in the integuments closed, but the internal wound never healed. The tumour increased with great encumbrance and very frequent pain, so tender as scarcely to endure any bandage, and so much inflamed as to threaten great mischief.

Such was my misery when I consulted Mr Mudge, and was driven back to town. Mr Pot found the danger not immediate but seemed to think excision unavoidable; but being to take a journey delayed it. While he was away the external wound burst open, and by very frequent effusions the tension is eased, the inflammation abated, and the protuberance so diminished as to incommode me very little, and scarcely to remind me of my disease by any pain.

Mr Pot upon re-examination thinks it best, since Nature has done so much, to look quietly on, and see what it will do more. I proposed another orifice, which I think Mr Cruikshank seems to approve, but Mr Pot thinks not proper. The operation is therefore at least suspended, the tumour is found not scirrous, and therefore not likely to corrupt any other part; and, says Pot, one would not carry "fire and sword further than is necessary".

I shall consult Mr Mudge, whose eagerness you know, and of whose judgement I think with great esteem, and enquire whether this new view of the case reconciles him to delay. . . .

227. *To Mrs. Thrale, Bath*

October 27, 1783

Madam . . .

Mrs. Siddons in her visit to me behaved with great modesty and propriety, and left nothing behind her to be censured or despised. Neither praise nor money, the two great corrupters of mankind, seem to have depraved her. I shall be pleased to see her again. Her brother Kemble calls on me, and pleases me very well. Mrs. Siddons and I talked of plays; and she told me her intention of exhibiting this winter the characters of Constance, Catherine, and Isabella in Shake-speare.[18]

I have had this day a letter from Mr. Mudge; who, with all his earnestness for operation, thinks it better to wait the effects of time, and, as he says, to let well alone. To this the patient naturally inclines . . .

228. To Sir Joshua Reynolds

December 4, 1783

Dear Sir

It is inconvenient to me to come out, I should else have waited on You with an account of a little evening club which we are establishing in Essex Street in the Strand, and of which You may be sure that You are desired to be one. It will be held at the Essex head now kept by an old Servant of Thrale's. The Company is numerous, and as You will be able to see by the list miscellaneous. The terms are lax, and the expences light. Mr Barry was adopted by Dr Brocklesby who joined with me in forming the plan. We meet thrice a week, and he who misses, forfeits two-pence.

If You are willing to become a Member, draw a line under your name. Return the list. We meet for the first time on Monday at eight.

I am Sir
Your most humble Servant
Sam: Johnson

229. To Mrs. Thrale, Bath

December 27, 1783

Dear Madam . . .

You have more than once wondered at my complaint of solitude, when you hear that I am crowded with visits. Inopem me copia fecit.[19] Visitors are no proper companions in the chamber of sickness.

[18] Constance in *King John*, Catherine in *Henry VIII*, Isabella in *Measure for Measure*.
[19] "Plenty has made me poor." (Ovid.)

They come when I could sleep, or read, they stay till I am weary, they force me to attend, when my mind calls for relaxation, and to speak when my powers will hardly actuate my tongue. The amusements and consolations of languor and depression are conferred by familiar and domestick companions, which can be visited or called at will, and can occasionally be quitted or dismissed, who do not obstruct accommodation by ceremony, or destroy indolence by awakening effort.

Such society I had with Levet and Williams, such I had where— I am never likely to have it more.[20]

I wish, dear Lady, to you and my dear Girls, many a cheerful and pious Christmas.

I am Your most &c
Sam: Johnson.

[20] Streatham.

1784

The last year of Johnson's life was marked above all things else by his continuing progress toward death; as he answered to a friend's inquiry after his health, "Sir, you cannot conceive with what acceleration I advance towards death." In *1781* he had lost Thrale; in *1782* Levett, his companion of thirty-eight years; in *1783* Miss Williams. In July of this year came the most bitter and violent of ruptures, his break with Mrs. Thrale. By this ugly separation an old man was left alone with his four fatal diseases, and life began to drain from one of its most ardent admirers.

The first four months of the year he spent confined to his sickroom in Bolt Court off Fleet Street, where he had been since early November. He was up and about, however, in May and June, and hoping, hoping in vain, that a new government grant, an "advance"

on his pension, would enable him to visit Italy in search of sunshine
and health. He saw Boswell for the last time on June 22; endured
Mrs. Thrale's "ignominious" remarriage; and left in July for the last
of his pilgrimages to Lichfield, Ashbourne, Birmingham, and Oxford.
He returned to London on November 16, a dying man.

230. To John Nichols

February 4, 1784

Mr Johnson having been for many weeks confined, is very cheerless, and wishes that when Mr. Nichols would now and then bestow
an hour upon him

231. To Mrs. Thrale, Bath

March 20, 1784

Madam . . .

Write to me no more about *dying with a grace*. When you feel
what I have felt in approaching Eternity—in fear of soon hearing
the sentence of which there is no revocation, you will know the
folly, my wish is that you may know it sooner. The distance between the grave and the remotest point of human longevity is but a
very little, and of that little no part is certain. You know all this,
and I thought that I knew it too, but I know it now with a new
conviction. May that new conviction not be vain. . . .

232. To John Taylor, Ashbourne

April 12, 1784

Dear Sir

What can be the reason that I hear nothing from you? I hope
nothing disables you from writing. What I have seen, and what I
have felt, gives me reason to fear every thing. Do not omit giving me
the comfort of knowing that after all my losses I have yet a friend
left.

I want every comfort. My Life is very solitary and very cheerless.
Though it has pleased God wonderfully to deliver me from the

Dropsy, I am yet very weak, and have not passed the door since the
13th of December. I hope for some help from warm weather, which
will surely come in time.

I could not have the consent of the Physicians to go to Church
yesterday; I therefore received the holy Sacrament at home, in the
room where I communicated with dear Mrs Williams a little before her death. O, my Friend, the approach of Death is very dreadful. I am afraid to think on that which I know, I cannot avoid. It is
vain to look round and round, for that help which cannot be had.
Yet we hope and hope, and fancy that he who has lived to day may
live to morrow. But let us learn to derive our hope only from God.

In the mean time, let us be kind to one another. I have no Friend
now living but You and Mr Hector that was the friend of my youth.
Do not neglect, dear Sir,

Yours affectionately,

Easter Monday   *Sam: Johnson*

233. *To Mrs. Thrale, Bath*

April 21, 1784

Dear Madam

I make haste to send you intelligence which if I do not still flatter
myself, you will not receive without some degree of pleasure. After
a confinement of one hundred twenty nine days, more than the third
part of a year, and no inconsiderable part of human life, I this day
returned thanks to God in St. Clement's Church, for my recovery,
a recovery in my seventy fifth year from a distemper which few in
the vigour of youth are known to surmount; a recovery of which
neither myself, my friends, nor my physicians had any hope, for
though they flattered me with some continuance of life, they never
supposed that I could cease to be dropsical. The Dropsy however, is
quite vanished, and the Asthma so much mitigated, that I walked to-
day with a more easy respiration than I have known, I think, for perhaps two years past. I hope the Mercy that lengthens my days, will
assist me to use them well.

The Hooles, Miss Burney, and Mrs. Hall (Wesly's sister) feasted
yesterday with me very cheerfully on your noble salmon. Mr. Allen

could not come, and I sent him a piece, and a great tail is still left.

Dr. Brocklesby forbids the club at present, not caring to venture the chillness of the evening but I purpose to shew myself on Saturday at the Academy's feast. I cannot publish my return to the world more effectually, for, as the Frenchman says, *tout le monde s'y trouvera.*[1]

For this occasion I ordered some cloaths, and was told by the taylor, that when he brought me a sick dress, he never expected to make me any thing of any other kind. My recovery is indeed wonderful.

I am, dear Madam,
Your most humble servant
Sam: Johnson

234. To Jane Langton, Rochester

May 10, 1784

My dearest Miss Jenny[2]

I am sorry that your pretty Letter has been so long without being answered; but when I am not pretty well, I do not always write plain enough for young Ladies.

I am glad, my Dear, to see that you write so well, and hope that you mind your pen, your book, and your needle, for they are all necessary. Your books will give you knowledge, and make you respected, and your needle will find you useful employment when you do not care to read. When you are a little older, I hope you will be very diligent in learning arithmetick; and above all, that through your whole life, you will carefully say your prayers, and read your Bible.

I am, my Dear
Your most humble servant,
Sam: Johnson.

[1] "Everyone will be there."
[2] She was eight years old, and Johnson's god-daughter.

1784

235. To Mrs. Thrale, Bath

July 2, 1784

Madam

If I interpret your letter right, you are ignominiously married, if it is yet undone, let us once talk together.[3] If you have abandoned your children and your religion, God forgive your wickedness; if you have forfeited your Fame, and your country, may your folly do no further mischief.

If the last act is yet to do, I, who have loved you, esteemed you, reverenced you, and served you, I who long thought you the first of human kind, entreat that before your fate is irrevocable, I may once more see you. I was, I once was,

Madam, most truly yours.
Sam: Johnson.

I will come down if you permit it.

236. To Mrs. Thrale, Bath

July 8, 1784

Dear Madam

What you have done, however I may lament it, I have no pretence to resent, as it has not been injurious to me. I therefore breathe out one sigh more of tenderness perhaps useless, but at least sincere.

I wish that God may grant you every blessing, that you may be happy in this world for its short continuance, and eternally happy in a better state. and whatever I can contribute to your happiness, I am very ready to repay for that kindness which soothed twenty years of a life radically wretched.

Do not think slightly of the advice which I now presume to offer. Prevail upon Mr. Piozzi to settle in England. You may live here with more dignity than in Italy, and with more security. Your rank will be higher, and your fortune more under your own eye. I desire

[3] She was not in fact married to Piozzi until July 23; but a formal letter sent to Johnson, as one of her late husband's executors, on June 30, had left the event unclear. Disapproval of the match was universal, immediate, and extraordinarily cruel.

211

not to detail all my reasons; but every argument of prudence and interest is for England, and only some phantoms of imagination seduce you to Italy.

I am afraid, however, that my counsel is vain, yet I have eased my heart by giving it.

When Queen Mary took the resolution of sheltering herself in England, the Archbishop of St. Andrew's attempting to dissuade her, attended on her journey and when they came to the irremeable stream that separated the two kingdoms, walked by her side into the water, in the middle of which he seized her bridle, and with earnestness proportioned to her danger and his own affection, pressed her to return. The Queen went forward.—If the parallel reaches thus far; may it go no further. The tears stand in my eyes.

I am going into Derbyshire, and hope to be followed by your good wishes, for I am with great affection

Your most humble servant,

Sam: Johnson

Any letters that come for me hither, will be sent me.

237. *To the Reverend Thomas Bagshaw, Bromley*

July 12, 1784

Sir

Perhaps you may remember, that in the year 1753, you committed to the ground my dear wife. I now entreat your permission to lay a stone over her; and have sent the inscription, that, if you find it proper, you may signify your allowance.

You will do me a great favour by showing the place where she lies, that the stone may protect her remains.

Mr. Ryland will wait on you for the inscription, and procure it to be engraved. You will easily believe that I shrink from this mournful office. When it is done, if I have strength remaining, I will visit Bromley once again, and pay you part of that respect to which you have a right from,

Reverend Sir, your most humble servant,

Sam. Johnson.

238. To Hester Maria ("Queeney") Thrale, Brighthelmston

Ashbourne, August 12, 1784

Dear Madam,

Your last letter was received by me at this place, and being so remote from the other Guardians that I could not consult them, I knew not what answer to make.[4] I take it very kindly that you have written again, for I would not have you forget me, nor imagine that I forget you. Our kindness will last, I hope, longer than our lives. Whatever advice I can give you you may always require; for I love you, I loved your father, and I loved your Mother as long as I could.

At present, I have nothing to impress but these two maxims, which I trust you never will dismiss from your mind.

In every purpose, and every action, let it be your first care to please God, that awful and just God before whom you must at last appear, and by whose sentence all Eternity will be determined. Think frequently on that state which shall never have an end.

In matters of human judgement, and prudential consideration, consider the publick voice of general opinion as always worthy of great attention; remember that such practices can very seldom be right, which all the world has concluded to be wrong.

Obey God.   Reverence Fame.

Thus you will go safely through this life, and pass happily to the next.

I am glad that my two other dear Girls are well.

I am dearest Madam,
Your most humble servant
Sam: Johnson

---

[4] Queeney, now nineteen, had fled from her mother and her mother's "low" husband—as she esteemed him—to an aunt in Brighton, taking the younger sisters with her. She wrote to Johnson and to the other executors (co-guardians under her father's will) for their blessing.

239. To Sir Joshua Reynolds

Ashbourne, September 9, 1784

Dear Sir

I could not answer your letter before this day, because I went on the sixth to Chatsworth and did not come back till the post was gone.

Many words I hope are not necessary between you and me to convince you, what gratitude is excited in my heart, by the Chancellor's Liberality, and your kind offices.[5] I did not indeed expect that what was asked by the Chancellor would have been refused, but since it has, we will not tell that any thing has been asked.

I have enclosed a Letter to the Chancellor, which, when you have read it, you will be pleased to seal with a Head or other general seal, and convey it to him: had I sent it directly to him, I should have seemed to overlook the favour of your intervention.

My last letter told you of my advance in health, which, I think, in the whole still continues. Of the hydropick tumour there is now very little appearance: the Asthma is much less troublesome, and seems to remit something day after day. I do not despair of supporting an English winter.

At Chatsworth I met young Mr Burke, who led me very commodiously into conversation with the Duke and Dutchess.[6] We had a very good morning. The Diner was publick.

I am, Dear Sir, with great affection,

Your humble servant

Sam: Johnson

---

[5] The Lord Chancellor, Thurlow, had offered to "lend" Johnson (through Reynolds) five or six hundred pounds for the Italian trip, when his request to the King was refused.

[6] Of Devonshire.

240. *To Lord Thurlow*

Ashbourne, September 9, 1784

My Lord

After a long and attentive observation of Mankind, the generosity of your Lordship's offer, excites in me no less wonder than gratitude. Bounty, so liberally bestowed if my condition made it necessary, I should gladly receive, for to such a Mind who would not be proud to own his obligations? But it has pleased God to restore me such a measure of health, that if I should now appropriate so much of a fortune destined to do good I should not escape from myself the charge of advancing a false claim. My journey to the Continent though I once thought it necessary was never much encouraged by my Physicians, and I was very desirous that your Lordship be told of it by Sir Joshua Reynolds as an event very uncertain; for if I grew much better, I should not be willing, if much worse, I should not be able, to migrate.

Your Lordship was Solicited without my knowledge, but when I was told that you were pleased to honour me with your patronage, I did not expect to hear of a refusal. Yet as I had little time to form hopes, and have not rioted in imaginary opulence, this cold reception has been scarce a disappointment; and from your Lordship's kindness I have received a benefit which only Men like You can bestow, I shall live *mihi charior*[7] with a higher opinion of my own merit.

I am.

241. *To John Taylor, Ashbourne*

Lichfield, October 23, 1784

Dear Sir,

Coming down from a very restless night I found your letter which made me a little angry. You tell me that recovery is in my power. This indeed I should be glad to hear, if I could once believe it. But you mean to charge me with neglecting or opposing my own health. Tell me therefore what I do that hurts me, and what I neglect that

[7] "More valuable to myself."

would help me. Tell it as soon as you can. . . . I would do it the sooner for your desire, and I hope to do it now in no long time, but shall hardly do it here. I hope soon to be at London. Answer the first part of this letter immediately.

> I am, dear Sir,
>
> Your most humble servant,
>
> *Sam: Johnson.*

242. *To James Boswell, Edinburgh*

Lichfield, November 3, 1784

Dear Sir

I have this summer sometimes amended and sometimes relapsed, but upon the whole, have lost ground very much. My legs are extremely weak, and my breath very short, and the water is now encreasing upon me. In this uncomfortable state your letters used to relieve; what is the reason that I have them no longer? Are you sick, or are you sullen? Whatever be the reason, if it be less than necessity, drive it away, and of the short life that we have, make the best use for yourself and for your friends. . . . I am sometimes afraid that your omission to write has some real cause, and shall be glad to know that you are not sick, and that nothing ill has befallen dear Mrs. Boswell, or any of your family.

> I am, Sir, your, &c.
>
> *Sam. Johnson.*

243. *To Richard Greene, Lichfield*

December 2, 1784

Dear Sir

I have enclosed the epitaph for my Father, Mother, and Brother, to be all engraved on the large size, and laid in the Middle Isle in St. Michael's Church, which I request the Clergyman and the Church-wardens to permit.

The first care must be to find the exact place of interment, that the stone may protect the bodies. Then let the stone be deep, massy, and hard, and do not let the difference of ten pounds or more defeat our purpose.

I have enclosed ten pounds, and Mrs. Porter will pay you ten more, which I gave her for the same purpose. What more is wanted shall be sent, and I beg that all possible haste may be made, for I wish to have it done while I am yet alive. Let me know, dear Sir, that you receive this.

> I am, Sir, your most humble servant,
> *Sam. Johnson.*

244. *To Lucy Porter, Lichfield*

December 2, 1784

Dear Madam

I am very ill, and desire your prayers. I have sent Mr Green the epitaph, and a power to call on You for ten pounds.

I laid this summer a stone over Tetty in the chapel of Bromley in Kent. The Inscription is in Latin of which this is the English.

Here lie the remains of Elizabeth, descended from the ancient house of Jarvis at Peatling in Leicestershire; a Woman of beauty, elegance, ingenuity, and piety. Her first Husband was Henry Porter; her second, Samuel Johnson, who having loved her much, and lamented her long, laid this stone upon her.

She died in March. 1752.

That this is done, I thought it fit that You should know; what care will be taken of us, who can tell? May God pardon and bless us, for Jesus Christs sake. Amen.

> I am, Madam,
> Your most humble Servant
> *Sam: Johnson.*

Sir

I was not sure that I read
your figures right, and therefore
must trouble you to set down
in words how much of my pension
I can call for now, and
how much will be due to me
at Christmas. I am, Sir,

Your most humble Servant

Dec. 7. 1784   Sam. Johnson

245. To William Strahan

December 7, 1784

Sir

I was not sure that I read your figures right, and therefore must trouble You to set down in words how much of my pension I can call for now, and how much will be due to me at Christmas.

I am, Sir,
Your most humble servant
Sam: Johnson

246. To William Strahan

December 10, 1784

Sir

I am very unwilling to take the pains of writing, and therefore make use of another hand to desire that I may have whatever portion of my pension you can spare me with prudence and propriety.

I am Sir your humble Servant
Sam: Johnson

Three days later, he was dead.

CHRONOLOGY OF IMPORTANT DATES

1709   Samuel Johnson born, Lichfield, Staffordshire, September 18.

1719-26   Attended Lichfield Grammar School and Stourbridge Grammar School.

1728-29   Attended Pembroke College, Oxford, leaving without a degree.

1730-31   Deep fit of melancholy.
1731   Death of father, Michael Johnson.
1732   Served for one term as usher (junior master) at Market Bosworth School, Leicestershire.

1735   Translated Father Lobo's *Voyage to Abyssinia.* Married Mrs. Elizabeth (Tetty) Porter, July 9.
1736   Briefly operated a private school at Edial, Staffordshire, with six to eight pupils.
1737   Traveled to London in March with David Garrick. Writing his tragedy *Irene.*

1738	Working for Edward Cave on *The Gentleman's Magazine*. Friendship with Richard Savage.		
1740-43	Writing Parliamentary Debates for *The Gentleman's Magazine*.	1740	*Pamela*.
		1742	*The Dunciad*, revised version. *Joseph Andrews*. End of Walpole's political domination. Handel, *Messiah*.
1744	*An Account of the Life of Mr. Richard Savage*.		
1745	*Miscellaneous Observations on the Tragedy of Macbeth*.	1745-46	Jacobite invasion.
1747	*Plan of a Dictionary of the English Language*, addressed to Lord Chesterfield.	1747-48	*Clarissa*.
		1748	Hume, *Enquiry concerning Human Understanding*. Collins, *Odes*. Montesquieu, *L'Esprit des Lois*.
1749	*The Vanity of Human Wishes*. *Irene: A Tragedy* produced by Garrick.	1749	*Tom Jones*.
1750-52	*The Rambler*, 208 bi-weekly issues.	1751	"Elegy Written in a Country Church-yard."
		1751-74	*L'Encyclopédie*.
1752	Death of Tetty, March 28.		
1753-54	Contributions to Hawkesworth's *The Adventurer*.		
		1754	Jonathan Edwards, *Freedom of the Will*.
1755	*A Dictionary of the English Language*. The "celebrated letter" to Chesterfield. Oxford M.A. degree.	1755	The Lisbon earthquake.

Chronology of Important Dates

1756	Death of Hill Boothby. *Proposals for Printing the Dramatick Works of William Shakespeare.*	1756-63	The Seven Years' War with France (called The French and Indian War in America), marking the rise of the British Empire under Chatham.
1756-57	Editing *The Literary Magazine.*		
1759	Death of mother, Sarah Johnson, at eighty-nine. Melancholia. *The History of Rasselas, Prince of Abissinia.*	1759	*Candide.*
		1760	Accession of George III. Macpherson, *Fragments of Ancient Poetry* ("Ossian").
		1760-67	*Tristram Shandy.*
1762	Granted royal pension of 300 pounds a year for life.	1762	Rousseau, *Le Contrat Social.*
1763	Met James Boswell, May 16.	1763	John Wilkes and the *North Briton* scandal.
1764	Founding of The Club with Reynolds, Goldsmith, Burke, and others.	1764	Voltaire, *Dictionnaire Philosophique.*
1765	Beginning of friendship with the Thrales. Melancholia. Dublin LL.D.	1765	The Stamp Act. Percy, *Reliques of Ancient English Poetry.* Walpole, *The Castle of Otranto.*
		1766	*The Vicar of Wakefield.*
1767	Conversation with George III. *The Plays of William Shakespeare.*		
		1768	Founding of the Royal Academy under Reynolds. The Middlesex Election riots (John Wilkes). Sterne, *A Sentimental Journey.*

		1769	Garrick's Shakespeare Jubilee. Watt's steam engine.
		1769-70	Captain Cook's voyage to the South Sea.
1770	*The False Alarm.* Seriously ill.		
		1771	Smollett, *Humphry Clinker.* Mackenzie, *The Man of Feeling.*
1773	Revised edition of *Dictionary.* Tour of Scotland and the Hebrides with Boswell (August-November).	1773	Boston Tea Party. *She Stoops to Conquer.*
1774	Trip to Wales with Mr. and Mrs. Thrale. *The Patriot.*	1774	Death of Goldsmith. Chesterfield, *Letters to His Son.* Goethe, *Faust.*
1775	*A Journey to the Western Islands of Scotland. Taxation No Tyranny.* Oxford LL.D. Trip to France with Thrales (September-November).	1775	Burke, *Speech on Conciliation with the Colonies.* American War for Independence begins, April.
1776	Death of Harry Thrale, junior. Dinner with John Wilkes.	1776	*The Declaration of Independence. The Wealth of Nations.*
		1776-87	*The Decline and Fall of the Roman Empire.*
		1777	Chatterton, *Works. The School for Scandal.*
		1778	*Evelina.*
1779-81	*The Lives of the Poets.*	1779	*Dialogues concerning Natural Religion.*
		1780	Gordon Riots.
1781	Death of Henry Thrale.	1781	Surrender of Cornwallis at Yorktown. Kant, *Critique of Pure Reason.*

		1781-88 Rousseau, *Confessions.*
1782	Death of Robert Levett.	1782 Collapse of North ministry.
		Cowper, *Poems.*
1783	Paralytic stroke, June 17.	1783 Pitt's Reform Bill fails.
	Break with Mrs. Thrale, July.	Treaty of Versailles, recognizing the United States.
	Death of Miss Williams, September.	
	Threatened operation; confined to sickbed, December-April.	
1784	Johnson died, December 13.	
1786	Mrs. Thrale's *Anecdotes.*	1786 Burns, *Poems.*
1787	Sir John Hawkins' *Life of Johnson.*	1787 Mozart, *Don Giovanni.*
		1787-88 *The Federalist.*
		1788 Beginning of Warren Hastings Trial.
		1789 The French Revolution.
		Blake, *Songs of Innocence.*
		The Mutiny on the *Bounty.*
		1790 Burke, *Reflections on the Revolution in France.*
1791	Boswell's *Life of Johnson.*	1791 Paine, *The Rights of Man.*
		1792 The French Republic.
		1793 Assassination of Louis XVI and Marie Antoinette.
		1794 *Songs of Experience.*
		1798 *Lyrical Ballads.*
		1799 Napoleon named First Consul.

INDEX OF NAMES

Slight references to minor dinner party guests, authors of books, and the like are not noted. A few of the more famous names—Boswell, Burke, Hogarth, Pitt, Reynolds, etc.—are presumed not to need identification. References are to letters, not pages; a number in italics indicates a letter *to* the person.

Index of Names

BURKE, RICHARD His son. 239

BURNEY, DR. CHARLES The most celebrated English musical scholar of the 18th Century, and father of the novelist. His correspondence and long friendship with Johnson began with an unsolicited testimonial for *The Rambler*. *31*, *33*, 175

BURNEY, FANNY The noted young authoress of *Evelina* and *Cecelia*. She was, with Johnson, a prize member of Mrs. Thrale's "Streatham Circle," which is vividly described in her Diary. 172, 174, 182, 233

BUTE, JOHN STUART, 3RD EARL Prime Minister 1762-63, confidant of the Young George III. *52*, *53*, *54*

CADELL, THOMAS One of the London booksellers contracting for Johnson's *Lives*. 193

CALDWELL, SIR JAMES An Irish baronet. 67

CARMICHAEL, "POLL" One of Johnson's Bolt Court inmates after 1778. "Mrs. Thrale. 'How came she among you, Sir?' Dr. Johnson. 'Why I don't rightly remember, but we could spare her very well from us. Poll is a stupid slut.'" (Fanny Burney's *Diary*) 165

CARTER, ELIZABETH A "bluestocking" or intellectual female who worked with Johnson in the *Gentleman's Magazine* days, and remained his friend for fifty years. 27, 204

CASTIGLIONE, PRINCE GONZAGA DI Italian diplomat and guest at Streatham. 147

CAVE, EDWARD Editor of the *Gentleman's Magazine*, Johnson's first London employer. See page 12. *1*, *3*, *4*, *6*, *7*, 27

CAVENDISH, LORD JOHN Chancellor of the Exchequer in Rockingham's brief 1782 ministry, uncle of the Duke of Devonshire. 205

CHAMBERS, CATHERINE ("Kitty") Johnson's mother's maid of many years. 37, 43, 44, 45, 53

CHAMBERS, (SIR) ROBERT Distinguished lawyer, Professor of Law at Oxford, Principal of New Inn Hall; after 1774 Judge of the Superior Court of Bengal in India. Johnson visited him frequently at Oxford and consulted him on legal matters. 46, 51, *68*, *85*, 96, 113, 206, *215*

CHAMIER, ANTHONY M.P., Undersecretary of State, founding member of The Club. 155, 170

CHARLES, PRINCE (The Young Pretender) 105

CHARLOTTE, QUEEN 119

CHATTERTON, THOMAS The boy-poet of Bristol. See 141, n. 7. 141, 201

CHESTER, BISHOP OF Beilby Porteus, later Bishop of London. 204

CHESTERFIELD, PHILIP DORMER STANHOPE, 4TH EARL Lord Lieutenant of Ireland, briefly Secretary of State, author of the famous *Letters to His Son;* the original dedicatee and would-be patron of Johnson's Dictionary. *19*, 173

229

231

Index of Names

GEORGE III   47, 48, 52, 53, 67, 118, 119, 151, 152, 153, 155, 168, 170, 180, 181, 183

GOLDSMITH, OLIVER   65, 78, 92, 93, *94*, 112, 113, 142, 158, 215

GORDON, ALEXANDER GORDON, 3RD DUKE   Brother of Lord George ("Gordon Riots") Gordon. 182

GORDON, LORD GEORGE   See 180, n. 25. 180, 181

GREENE, RICHARD   Apothecary and antiquary of Lichfield. *243*, 244

GRENVILLE, GEORGE   Prime Minister from 1763-65, author of the famous Stamp Act of 1765. *56*

GREVILLE, RICHARD FULKE   Author of a book of maxims. M.P. from Wiltshire, minor member of a distinguished literary and political line. 175

HADRIAN   Quoted, 173

HAILES, LORD (SIR DAVID DALRYMPLE)   Scottish judge and man of letters. 121, 219

HALL, MRS. MARTHA   Sister of John and Charles Wesley. 136, 233

HAMILTON, WILLIAM GERARD   Member of Parliament ("Single-Speech Hamilton") under whom Burke served his political apprenticeship, and for whom Johnson wrote speeches. 175

HARDY, ADMIRAL SIR CHARLES   Commander of the Channel Fleet. 170

HARRINGTON, CAROLINE FITZROY, COUNTESS OF   Daughter of the Duke of Grafton, widow of the Earl of Harrington; a reigning beauty in her day, a notorious eccentric, friend of Horace Walpole. It was she who first asked Johnson to intercede in the Dodd case. *153*

HARRINGTON, HENRY   Fashionable physician of Bath. 141, 174

HARRIS, JAMES   Writer, Member of Parliament. 175

HASTINGS, WARREN   Governor-General of India. He was impeached for malfeasance in a spectacular trial that began in 1788. *192*, 215

HAWKESWORTH, DR. JOHN   A miscellaneous writer, editor, and early friend of Johnson's. He edited *The Adventurer.* 67

HAWKINS, SIR JOHN   Judge, author, and pre-Boswellian biographer of Johnson. Though a founding member of The Club, Johnson thought him "a very unclubable man." Boswell despised him. 65

HEBERDEN, DR. WILLIAM   One of Johnson's physicians in his last illness. 218, 219, 225

HECTOR, EDMUND   A schoolmate of Johnson's at Lichfield, nephew of the "mad-midwife" who delivered him, brother of his first love, and his closest childhood friend. He was a Birmingham surgeon. *30*, 232

HERNE, ELIZABETH   The lunatic daughter of Johnson's cousin. He shared with Mary Prowse the expense of her maintenance, and left a £100 legacy for her in his will. 191

HOGARTH, WILLIAM   83

HOLDER, ROBERT   London apothecary. 199

Index of Names

HOLLYER, JOHN   A cousin of Johnson's in Coventry. *117*

HOMER   Quoted, 88

HOOLE, JOHN   A clerk of the East India Company who translated *Orlando Furioso*. 67, 192, 204, 233

HORACE   Quoted, 93, 103

HOWARD, CHARLES   Lawyer of Lichfield, schoolmate of Johnson's. 44

HUGGINS, WILLIAMS   A translator of Ariosto and Dante, who had quarreled with Johnson and Baretti. 55

HUNTER, LUCY   Aunt of Lucy Porter. 44

HUNTER, WILLIAM   The Queen's physician, Professor of Anatomy at the Royal Academy, Fellow of the Royal Society. *118*, 119, 205

HUTTON, WILLIAM   A celebrated sectarian missionary. 182

JENKINSON, CHARLES   1ST EARL OF LIVERPOOL. A protégé of Lord Bute's, holder of several ministerial positions under Bute, North, and Pitt. *150, 152*

JOHNSON, ELIZABETH ("Tetty")   Johnson's wife. *5*, 15, 17, 196, 237, 244

JOHNSON, MICHAEL   Johnson's father. 243

JOHNSON, NATHANIEL   Johnson's younger brother (1712-1737). Very little is known of him. 191, 243

JOHNSON, SARAH   Johnson's mother. 5, 9, 15, 30, *36*, 37, *38, 39*, 40, *41*, 43, 44, 45, *243*

JOHNSON, THOMAS   Johnson's cousin. See Letter 117. 73, *117*

JOHNSTON, WILLIAM   London bookseller. 42

JONES, SIR WILLIAM   Lawyer and Oriental scholar. 215

KEMBLE, JOHN PHILIP   Celebrated actor, brother of the actress Sarah Siddons. 227

KNAPTON, PAUL or JOHN   London booksellers who were among the co-publishers of the Dictionary. 8

KNOWLES, MARY   "The ingenious Quaker lady" famed for her needlework; she was one of Johnson's less successful conversational antagonists. 141

KNOX, JOHN   100

LADE, LADY MARY   Sister of Henry Thrale. 182

LANGTON, BENNET   Twenty-eight years Johnson's junior, Langton became one of his closest friends. He was a great tavern-companion, and one of the original members of The Club. He married the widow of the Earl of Rothes, and settled into noisy domesticity with his nine children and his unpaid bills. *34, 35, 46*, 55, *65, 78, 113*, 121, *127*, 173, 175, *198, 202*, 215, 219, *225*

LANGTON, JANE   Langton's daughter, Johnson's goddaughter. *234*. There are references to Jane and the other Langton children in the letters to their father.

LAW, WILLIAM 18th Century religious writer. 26.

LAWRENCE, DR. THOMAS President of the Royal College of Surgeons, the most distinguished of Johnson's many physicians. He suffered a paralyzing stroke in 1782 more dire even than Johnson's, leaving him totally disabled until his death in June 1783. 23, 25, 35, 174, *199*, 207, 215, 218, 226.

LEE, ARTHUR ("Counsellor") A secret agent of the American Congress, and thus nearly as despicable to Johnson as Wilkes. 141

LEE, WILLIAM His brother, a London merchant and Alderman, also in the enemy's service. 141

LELAND, THOMAS One of the Senior Fellows of Trinity College, Dublin. *62*

LEVETT, ROBERT "An obscure practrioner in physick among the lower people," who shared Johnson's house and breakfast for over thirty years. His death in 1782 drew from Johnson a moving and eloquent tribute in verse. 51, 55, *134, 135, 144*, 165, 199, 202, 215, 220, 229.

LEWIS, JOHN Dean of Ossory, married Charlotte Cottrell. 55

LONGMAN, THOMAS One of the five contracting publishers for the Dictionary. *8*.

LOUIS XVI and QUEEN MARIE ANTOINETTE 135

LOWE, MAURITIUS A poor painter John sponsored. 216

LUCAN, MARGARET BINGHAM, COUNTESS OF London Society hostess and amateur painter. 175

LYE, REV. EDWARD Linguistic scholar. 65

MACDONALD, SIR ALEXANDER (and LADY ELIZABETH) A classic Scotch miser of Skie; one of Johnson's more frugal hosts. See page 100. 102, 103

MACDONALD, ALLAN Husband of Flora Macdonald, of Kingsburgh, Skie. They emigrated to North Carolina the year after Johnson's visit, but later returned to Scotland. 105

MACDONALD, FLORA Jacobite heroine of the '45 Invasion. See page 108. 105

MACLEAN, SIR ALLAN Chief of the Clan Maclean, reduced to dwelling in a thatched hut on the Island of Inch Kenneth. See pages 112-113. 107

MACLEAN, DONALD See Coll

MACLEOD, FLORA Daughter of Raasay, "a celebrated Beauty," 104

MACLEOD, JOHN, of Raasay, 9th Chief See Raasay

MACLEOD, COL. JOHN, of Talisker, and MRS. FLORENCE MACLEOD A Colonel in the Scots brigade in Holland. 105

MACLEOD, MALCOLM· Cousin of Raasay, a Jacobite partisan in the '45. 103, 105

MACLEOD, NORMAN, 20th Chief of the Clan Macleod, of Dunvegan, Skie;